"Nothing is more exciting—or more important—than the promises and prophecies of Scripture. Nothing brings greater hope. Nothing brings greater clarity to our lives. I thank the Lord, and my good friend Stan, for this encouraging and important piece of work."

Luis Palau, world evangelist; author of *Out of the Desert . . . Into the Life God Fully Intended*

"Stan Guthrie is a cogent thinker and graceful writer I love to read. While *A Concise Guide to Bible Prophecy* happens to cover an area of personal interest for me, Stan can draw me into any subject simply by the way he examines and explains it. Every Guthrie book is a treat."

Jerry B. Jenkins, novelist and biographer;
owner of Christian Writers Guild

"Bible prophecy is a subject that's often been smothered by fantasy, confusion, and outright distortion. Stan Guthrie addresses it with lucidity, humility, and a deep love for God's Word."

—John Wilson, editor, *Books and Culture*

A CONCISE GUIDE TO
Bible
Prophecy

60 PREDICTIONS
EVERYONE SHOULD KNOW

STAN GUTHRIE

BakerBooks

a division of Baker Publishing Group
Grand Rapids, Michigan

© 2013 by Stan Guthrie

Published by Baker Books
a division of Baker Publishing Group
P.O. Box 6287, Grand Rapids, MI 49516-6287
www.bakerbooks.com

Printed in the United States of America

Library of Congress Cataloging-in-Publication Data
Guthrie, Stan.
    A concise guide to Bible prophecy : 60 predictions everyone should know / Stan
Guthrie.
        pages cm
    Includes bibliographical references.
    ISBN 978-0-8010-1509-0 (pbk.)
    1. Bible—Prophecies. I. Title.
BS647.3.G88 2013
220.1′5—dc23   2012046706

The internet addresses, email addresses, and phone numbers in this book are accurate at the time of publication. They are provided as a resource. Baker Publishing Group does not endorse them or vouch for their content or permanence.

13 14 15 . 16 17 18 19   7 6 5 4 3 2 1

To Mom and Dad:
Irene S. Guthrie and S. Morris Guthrie

Grace to you and peace
from God our Father and
the Lord Jesus Christ.

I thank my God in all
my remembrance of you . . .
making my prayer with joy.

Contents

The Once and Future Kings

Jesus—First Advent

Jesus—Life and Ministry

Jesus—Death and Resurrection

The Church

Last Days, Second Advent, and the Final State

Introduction

When I was new to the Bible, the subject of prophecy fascinated me—and, to tell the truth, it still does. I was constantly scanning the headlines for confirmation of scriptural predictions about the future. Was the restoration of the State of Israel a harbinger of the "End Times"? Were developments in Western Europe precursors of a "revived Roman Empire"? Could we calculate the date of Christ's return?

In our search to know what is to come, many of us turn to the Bible for answers, because its ultimate author (God) claims to know the end from the beginning. Both the Hebrew Scriptures (Old Testament) and the Christian New Testament are loaded with prophets and prophecies.

Think of the word *prophet*, and you're likely to come up with quite a range of characters. Nostradamus, Jeane Dixon, Isaiah from the Old Testament, and Edgar Cayce may come to mind just for starters. There are many people who claim to know the future. Some wear long, burlap robes and carry signs proclaiming "The end is near," while others who wear pinstripes and Guccis urge us to buy gold in preparation for the "coming economic catastrophe."

We saw this dynamic yet again in the recent frenzy over Harold Camping, some of whose followers spent their life savings to rent billboards to warn the world about the rapture and the end of the world. Camping's apocalyptic predictions of the return of Christ, of course, like those of countless others before him, failed to come to pass, inviting depression in some and mockery from others.

But Camping's tragic errors no more invalidate biblical prophecy than someone refusing to double-check a driving route invalidates the global positioning system device on the car dashboard. The value of prophecy stands. It is up to us to figure out how to use it so we can get to where God wants us to go. That's what this little book is about.

Bible scholars say that the prophets are God's spokesmen (and women), who both *foretell* what is ahead and *forth tell* what we are to do now. Technically, *every* statement in the Bible can be classified as *prophecy*—as a word from God (2 Pet. 1:20–21). But in this guide we will confine the meaning of a biblical prophecy to *a statement by God or his representative concerning the future.* And for a prophecy to be confirmed as ultimately from *God* rather than from mere men and women (2 Tim. 3:16), the test is straightforward and unyielding. According to Moses, the prophecy *must come true* (Deut. 18:21–22). When it comes to prophecy, God does not grade on a curve.

The Bible, written over a period of nearly 1,500 years and covering events from creation to the end of the world and beyond, has hundreds and hundreds of predictive prophecies—of numerous literary types—within its pages. Christian apologist Hugh Ross suggests that some 2,500 prophecies appear in the Bible—with 500 still awaiting fulfillment[1]—but only God knows the true number. Either they have already come to pass (some in multiple stages) or they await a future fulfillment. (And some that have already been fulfilled partially in history await a final, complete fulfillment when the world is made new.)

Some prophecies are crystal clear both in their presentation and in their fulfillment, such as the prediction in the book of Micah that the Messiah would be born in Bethlehem. Others, such as the return of the boy Jesus and his family from Egypt, are best seen in hindsight. Yet all give us important information about God, the world . . . and ourselves.

A little bit about me and the method I use in this volume:

- I believe the Bible is the inspired Word of God. This means that it comes *from* God, *through* human agency (again, see 2 Peter 1:20–21). As a divine-human product, however, the Bible uses cultural and literary forms that, while communicating truth about God, humanity, or the world, cannot always be taken *literally.* For example, it assumes the perspectives common to earthbound readers—such as portraying that the sun rises in the east and sets in the west. Metaphor is a common literary device. When Jesus says, "I am the door" (John 10:9), he is clearly using one. No one expects to find a doorknob or hinges protruding from the Savior's robe.
- I believe that Scripture, as originally written, contains no errors. Unprecedented levels of study over the centuries, by friend and foe alike, have only confirmed this belief. Though no original

manuscripts of God's Word remain, we have thousands of copies (some of which were made within mere decades of the originals), bolstering our confidence that the Bible we possess has not been changed in any significant way. No other ancient manuscript comes close to this level of attestation, and the basic truth of Scripture has been confirmed by archaeology and other sources of knowledge again and again.[2]

• I believe this little volume you hold in your hands (or on your e-reader) will show that all of Scripture—and all of prophecy—ultimately points to Christ. As the risen Lord told some of his disciples: "O foolish ones, and slow of heart to believe all that the prophets have spoken! Was it not necessary that the Christ should suffer these things and enter into his glory?" Then we have this statement from Luke: "And beginning with Moses and all the Prophets, he interpreted to them in all the Scriptures the things concerning himself" (Luke 24:25–27). Ultimately, prophecy points to Jesus Christ.

In *A Concise Guide to Bible Prophecy*, we will look at sixty key prophecies in the Bible, each through the lens of one or several Bible verses. Although only a small fraction of the total, these predictions are representative of the whole. Taken together, they enable us to grasp the main themes of Scripture, and they lay a solid foundation for additional study.

I make no claim that this slim work will cover such a grand subject exhaustively, but it will help us see how the prophecies fit together in the overall sweep of Scripture. It will also help us avoid the common pitfall of wresting individual prophecies from their contexts, an error that causes many readers to go astray when interpreting the Bible's predictions.

To enhance our understanding and to avoid misinterpretation to the best of our ability, we will consider these prophecies by category, in the context of the rest of God's Word as well as any applicable historical events. That's because the prophecies were given *by* real people *to* real people *in* real historical situations and *facing* real issues.

Following your own interests, feel free to read the chapters in any order you desire. Each is written to stand on its own. However, I believe you will get the most from this book if you read about the prophecies in order, as I have arranged them. I believe this approach will best illuminate the key themes of Scripture and the unfolding of salvation history.

To aid you in further studying this vital subject, in the back of the book are some basic principles of hermeneutics (biblical interpretation) and the main approaches that Christians (including me) use when handling prophecy and studying the end of the world (eschatology).

This book is not a dry, academic discussion about prophecy. Nor is it a sensationalistic attempt to tickle our fancy about the future. Instead, it is meant to help, instruct, and encourage ordinary people like you and me. It aims to create or strengthen belief in the Bible as God's Word. My hope is that it will give you a deeper appreciation for the unity and genius of Scripture; trust in the omnipotent, omniscient God who is unstoppably at work in human history; and an unshakable confidence about the future. Toward that final goal, this book will offer a personal application for each prophecy.

Just as the Bible's many predictions had meaning for their hearers when they were initially given, so they have significance for us today— whether the events they describe have already happened or still await a future fulfillment. That's because prophecy is never given solely to satisfy our curiosity about what is to come. It is also meant to transform our lives *today*. As 2 Peter 3:1–2 says, "I am stirring up your sincere mind by way of reminder, that you should remember the predictions of the holy prophets and the commandment of the Lord and Savior."

So let's get started.

Israel

1

Blessed to Be a Blessing

Genesis 12:1–3

God calls an unknown man named Abram out of Ur of the Chaldeans, a sophisticated pagan society of moon worshipers, to wander in an unknown land.

> Now the LORD said to Abram, "Go from your country and your kindred and your father's house to the land that I will show you. And I will make of you a great nation, and I will bless you and make your name great, so that you will be a blessing. I will bless those who bless you, and him who dishonors you I will curse, and in you all the families of the earth shall be blessed."
>
> Genesis 12:1–3

The fulfillment of this four-thousand-year-old promise, like so many other prophecies, occurs on more than one level. First, of course, the "great nation" is fulfilled in Israel and the Jewish people, who bless the world with their presence on the strategic land bridge connecting Europe, Asia, and Africa. Abram and his wife, Sarai (later, Abraham and Sarah), battle decades of doubt and desperation before miraculously receiving Isaac, their son and heir, from God.

Sadly Isaac's son (Abraham's grandson) Jacob is forced from the land of promise because of his own greed and trickery. Is the prophecy to Abram nullified? Not at all, because by God's grace Jacob is restored to the land with his sons, who will become heads of the twelve tribes of Israel. These men, however, jealous of their gifted and conceited brother,

Joseph, sell him into Egyptian slavery. But Joseph grows in his faith and in his position, rising to become second-in-command in the nation. His God-given wisdom and prophetic foresight enable Egypt to thrive in the midst of a massive famine.

Jacob and his family (including Joseph's evil brothers) are forced to flee the Promised Land for Egypt to survive the famine. Is the prophecy of Genesis 12:1–3 then overturned? No, as the Lord will again bring his people back and establish them in the land (see chapter 3, "Deliverance from Egypt"). Subsequently the kings and nations that bless Israel will be blessed, and those that oppose the vehicle of God's salvation program will face judgment.

Eventually Israel, despite many highlights of faithfulness, fails in its mission. God judges his people accordingly, using the nations of Assyria and Babylon to bring down the Jewish kingdom. Only a remnant is eventually brought back to the land. Israel's glory days are over, apparently forever. What then of the prophesied promise to Abraham and his "offspring"?

The New Testament says that ultimately the prophecy looks ahead to Jesus Christ, Israel's Messiah and the world's Redeemer, and his followers of every nation. In the age of Rome, Jesus tells the discouraged nation about the ultimate kingdom of God. We see this new chapter of salvation history begin in a dramatic way on the day of Pentecost, forty days after the resurrection of Jesus, when the Holy Spirit is poured out on an international gathering of Jews in Jerusalem (Acts 2) and then on the Gentiles (Acts 10), who become "Abraham's offspring, heirs according to promise" (Gal. 3:29).

The prophecy that Abraham and all God's people are blessed to be a blessing is also a command. The resurrected Christ's Great Commission crystallizes our joyous responsibility for the world: "All authority in heaven and on earth has been given to me. Go therefore and make disciples of all nations, baptizing them in the name of the Father and of the Son and of the Holy Spirit, teaching them to observe all that I have commanded you. And behold, I am with you always, to the end of the age" (Matt. 28:18–20).

APPLICATION

**God's blessings are worth waiting for,
and they are to be shared.**

2

Jacob Returns

Genesis 28:13–15

In the Old Testament, God's work of blessing the nations centers around Israel living out biblical faith in the Promised Land, pointing the surrounding pagan cultures to the one true God. Jacob, Abraham's grandson, is to become the father of this nation.

Jacob (which means "supplanter") is the twin (and younger) brother of Esau and emerges from the womb holding Esau's heel. Later, Jacob, with the help of his scheming mother, Rebekah, conspires to deceive his aging father, Isaac, and steal Esau's blessing. Esau, already impetuous and hotheaded, is quite naturally enraged and vows to kill Jacob, who flees into the wilderness, fearing for his life.

The night of his escape, Jacob lies down exhausted on the hard ground to catch some desperately needed sleep. His departure has been so abrupt that the only thing he has for a pillow is a stone. Somehow, uneasily, he drifts off to dreamland. Suddenly he is confronted with a vision of a ladder that reaches from heaven to earth, with angels ascending and descending on it. Then he hears the voice of God.

> The land on which you lie I will give to you and to your offspring. Your offspring shall be like the dust of the earth, and you shall spread abroad to the west and to the east and to the north and to the south, and in you and your offspring shall all the families of the earth be blessed. Behold, I am with you and will keep you wherever you go, and will

bring you back to this land. For I will not leave you until I have done what I have promised you.

Genesis 28:13–15

Immediately Jacob realizes that this is not just any dream but a prophecy from the Almighty: "Then Jacob awoke from his sleep and said, 'Surely the LORD is in this place, and I did not know it'" (v. 16).

In this message God reiterates to the grandson (Jacob) what he already promised the grandfather (Abraham)—that he will be blessed to be a blessing. Yet how can this be, since Jacob is on his way to pagan territory, where he will spend many long years?

God's blessing actually follows Jacob to his Uncle Laban's home. Like the mythical King Midas, everything Jacob touches turns to gold. Eventually, laden with riches and a growing family, a slowly maturing Jacob leaves Laban and heads back to the Promised Land, uncertain of his future. But God remains with him, and Jacob's hard-won faith (and some well-timed gifts to Esau) precede his reinstatement to the land of blessing.

Yet in his old age, famine strikes, and Jacob and his growing clan are forced to pull up stakes and head to Egypt as a matter of survival. The land is again bereft of God's people. Has the prophecy pronounced in a dream so many years before finally failed? No, because Jacob knows he will eventually return to his homeland. But for now the Jewish people go with him to the land of Pharaoh, where they flourish and multiply, becoming a mighty nation.

Before he dies in Egypt, ancient Jacob gets his exalted son, Joseph, to promise to take his bones from Egypt to the Promised Land, which the great leader does after winning approval from Pharaoh: "So Joseph went up to bury his father. With him went up all the servants of Pharaoh, the elders of his household, and all the elders of the land of Egypt" (50:7). Jacob, once the trickster, does not want to miss out on the worldwide blessing that he knows is coming. In faithful death, Jacob is literally re-deposited in the land of promise, a down payment on all that is to come.

APPLICATION

**Even when we fail, we can count on
God's promises.**

3

Deliverance from Egypt

Exodus 6:1

After Joseph passes from the scene, the good times in Egypt come to a screeching halt for the Jewish people.

> Now there arose a new king over Egypt, who did not know Joseph. And he said to his people, "Behold, the people of Israel are too many and too mighty for us. Come, let us deal shrewdly with them, lest they multiply, and, if war breaks out, they join our enemies and fight against us and escape from the land." Therefore they set taskmasters over them to afflict them with heavy burdens. They built for Pharaoh store cities, Pithom and Raamses. But the more they were oppressed, the more they multiplied and the more they spread abroad. And the Egyptians were in dread of the people of Israel. So they ruthlessly made the people of Israel work as slaves and made their lives bitter with hard service, in mortar and brick, and in all kinds of work in the field. In all their work they ruthlessly made them work as slaves.
>
> Exodus 1:8–14

At this point, God's prophecies to the patriarchs seem like a cruel joke. Yes, Israel is now a "great nation," but it is also a hopelessly enslaved people. Yet God's plan isn't frustrated, and he continues patiently to work out his purposes for the world. At the right time, hundreds of years later, he raises up a man, Moses, from Pharaoh's own household to lead the people back to the land of promise. Proud Pharaoh, however, has a hardened heart and refuses to let them go.

So God, working through Moses, demonstrates his sovereign power. He performs a series of miraculous plagues, from flies that cover the land to blood that contaminates the water. Each time, Pharaoh initially agrees to let the Jewish people go before going back on his word, relying on the false power of the Egyptian gods.

Finally, the Lord reassures a discouraged Moses: "Now you shall see what I will do to Pharaoh; for with a strong hand he will send them out, and with a strong hand he will drive them out of his land" (6:1). This prophecy seems impossible, but Pharaoh, facing the ultimate calamity, the loss of all the firstborn in Egypt (including his own son), actually *orders* God's people out (12:31–36).

However, the king of Egypt changes his mind once again and sends his chariots after the Israelites to slaughter them by the sea. But God parts the Red Sea for the Jews; the Egyptians, heedless of the danger, plunge into the breach after them.

> Then the LORD said to Moses, "Stretch out your hand over the sea, that the water may come back upon the Egyptians, upon their chariots, and upon their horsemen." So Moses stretched out his hand over the sea, and the sea returned to its normal course when the morning appeared. And as the Egyptians fled into it, the LORD threw the Egyptians into the midst of the sea. The waters returned and covered the chariots and the horsemen; of all the host of Pharaoh that had followed them into the sea, not one of them remained. But the people of Israel walked on dry ground through the sea, the waters being a wall to them on their right hand and on their left.
>
> Exodus 14:26–29

So Pharaoh has again reneged—but for the last time. It is time for the prophecy to be fulfilled—without him. Pharaoh is ultimately an unwilling participant in God's prophecy . . . but a participant nonetheless. God's plan to bless the world through his people marches on.

APPLICATION

**God's promises may seem long in coming
but they always prove true.**

4

Blessings and Curses

Deuteronomy 28

On November 1, 1755, a cataclysmic earthquake strikes Lisbon. When it is over, more than ninety thousand people in Portugal are dead. Another ten thousand die in Spain and Morocco. In Voltaire's *Candide*, the title character watches from Lisbon harbor as the good perish and the evil survive.[1]

With every natural disaster since, from Krakatoa to the Asian tsunami, people have asked why bad things happen to good people—always assuming that *they* are among the good. Like petulant children, we are quick to claim, "It's not fair!" when we face hardship or death. "If only God would treat us as we deserve!"

In one era of history, God seemingly did just that—among the Jewish people. (Actually the surrounding pagan nations were also included in God's program to give people what they deserved.) In that far distant era, God's desire was to inculcate values and behaviors necessary to make his people truly his and to use them as a model to draw the surrounding peoples to himself.

But while the Lord would show his grace (unmerited favor) to the Jews and the other peoples, he would also show his severe justice. Before the Jews could receive the Promised Land as a staging area to bless the nations, the corrupt locals—called Amorites—would have to be removed. Turning their backs on the knowledge of the one God, they had turned to paganism, child sacrifice, and countless forms of brutality. Accordingly they *deserved* his judgment.

Yet even here God is gracious, telling Abraham more than six hundred years before the coming conquest, "the iniquity of the Amorites is not yet complete" (Gen. 15:16). In the intervening centuries, the locals receive ample opportunities to repent, but refuse. So the Jewish people roll in from Egypt and bring God's righteous judgment.

The same principle of grace and justice is at work in the life of God's people, who must be holy if they are to bless the world. Through Moses, God prophesies to his people: "And if you faithfully obey the voice of the LORD your God, being careful to do all his commandments that I command you today, the LORD your God will set you high above all the nations of the earth" (Deut. 28:1).

And at various times, God's blessings are evident. Faith, heroism, and other virtues flourish in Israel. The nations begin to see God's glory through this small window in the Middle East. Ruth of Moab joins Israel and becomes an ancestor of the promised Messiah. As the kingdom begins and prospers, the surrounding people come to Israel, which is strategically situated at the crossroads of the world—where Europe, Asia, and Africa meet. Among the visitors to God's kingdom and temple are Hiram of Tyre and the Queen of Sheba, who seeks Solomon's wisdom.

Yet the blessings do not last for God's people. Iniquity resides in the hearts of these "sons of Adam and daughters of Eve," and they rebel against their Lord and against each other, eventually splitting into two kingdoms. So their blessings turn into curses, as predicted by Moses: "And you shall become a horror, a proverb, and a byword among all the peoples where the LORD will lead you away" (v. 37).

Despite repeated and ever-increasing warnings from God's prophets, his people choose to ignore him. The land groans under their idolatry, greed, and violence and eventually expels them. The results are summarized in 2 Kings 25. First, Israel, the Northern Kingdom, is carried off to Assyria. Then Judah, in the south, succumbs to Babylon. They are scattered to the four winds, removed from the Promised Land.

God's people get what they deserve.

APPLICATION

God's justice and grace go together.

5

Elijah's Drought

1 Kings 17:1

Sometimes we think that if we obey God, if we take a step of faith, everything will be easy. The story of Elijah, the prophet who stood against Ahab, Jezebel, and pagan religion in the Northern Kingdom, tells us otherwise.

King Ahab, under the malicious influence of his Phoenician wife, Jezebel, "did evil in the sight of the LORD, more than all who were before him" (1 Kings 16:30). So God sent a prophet named Elijah to warn him of God's impending curse on the land. "As the LORD, the God of Israel, lives, before whom I stand," Elijah announces, "there shall be neither dew nor rain these years, except by my word" (17:1). It is a direct challenge to the pagan religion of Baal, who was believed to control fertility.[1]

As predicted, the rain stops and the brooks dry up. It's not surprising that Elijah is forced to hide from Ahab and Jezebel, who hope for revenge. Years later God sends Elijah back to the king, who is beside himself over the continuing drought. Elijah orchestrates a confrontation with 450 prophets of Baal on parched Mount Carmel. Will the people of God choose the Lord or Baal?

On the appointed day, two altars are built, with a bull placed on each one for sacrifice, but no fire is lighted. Elijah says, "the God who answers by fire, he is God" (18:24).

After frenzied and exhausting pleading, the priests of Baal fail to rouse their god. Then Elijah stands before the altar of the Lord and prays, "O

LORD, God of Abraham, Isaac, and Israel, let it be known this day that you are God in Israel, and that I am your servant, and that I have done all these things at your word. Answer me, O LORD, answer me, that this people may know that you, O LORD, are God, and that you have turned their hearts back" (vv. 36–37).

God answers his prophet dramatically. The "fire of the Lord" comes crashing down, the false priests are wiped out, and the people return to God—at least for a time. Then Elijah, atop the mountain, prays for rain and sees "a little cloud like a man's hand . . . rising from the sea" (v. 44). Soon a terrific storm arrives, and the drought is over. It is a remarkable triumph for God—and for the prophet Elijah, "a man with a nature like ours" (James 5:17).

Yet Ahab and Jezebel are not celebrating. The evil couple seeks to murder Elijah once and for all. Now it is time for *Elijah* to be exhausted. After seeing God answer all his prayers and prophecies, Elijah has what can only be called a bout of spiritual depression. In terror he flees for his life and asks God to put him out of his misery, saying (inaccurately), "I, even I only, am left" (1 Kings 19:10). A man who has controlled the weather, pronounced judgment, and sparked a great revival has come crashing down to earth.

In a series of events that are both awesome and spiritually encouraging, the Lord appears to his wounded prophet and assures him he is not alone and that there is still work to do (vv. 11–19). Elijah picks himself up, wiser now, and completes his assignment. The God who holds the fate of the nations in his hands has a steady shoulder for his people to lean on in times of great stress.

APPLICATION

**God will be with us in the good times
and the bad.**

6

Judgment against Israel

Hosea 9:3; Amos 3:11–12

The Golden Age of Solomon has brought renown and wealth to the Jewish state. The magnificent temple to the Lord, where God reigns in the midst of his people, is built according to the Lord's exacting specifications. The surrounding nations, exemplified by the Queen of Sheba, are drawn to the king's wisdom.

"Your wisdom and prosperity surpass the report that I heard," she exclaims. "Happy are your men! Happy are your servants, who continually stand before you and hear your wisdom! Blessed be the LORD your God, who has delighted in you and set you on the throne of Israel!" (1 Kings 10:7–9).

God's horticultural project of blessing Israel to bless the nations is bearing fruit—but a bitter root threatens to poison everything. In the final years of his reign, Solomon becomes more like a common Middle Eastern despot than God's representative on earth. He allows his wives, many of them worshipers of the surrounding nations' gods, to set up false shrines. To carry out his immense building projects, Solomon resorts to heavy taxation and forced conscription.

When Solomon dies, the kingdom falls to his son Rehoboam. Facing demands for leniency, the son boasts, "My father disciplined you with whips, but I will discipline you with scorpions" (12:14). So Israel splits, with the permission of God.

The ruler of the new kingdom in the north, which appropriates the name Israel, is the similarly named Jeroboam. Israel retains ten of the original dozen Jewish tribes. The remnant kingdom in the south retains two—Judah and Benjamin—and is named Judah. Significantly, the Southern Kingdom retains the temple and the royal line of David, Solomon's father.

Tragically, Jeroboam, to consolidate his power, institutes syncretistic religious worship, defying God's law. Thus begin two centuries of idolatry in the Northern Kingdom. Idolatry begets greed, oppression, and all manner of social ills. God responds by sending prophets calling for reform, but all of Israel's kings indulge unrepentantly in what the Bible calls "the sin of the house of Jeroboam" (13:34 NIV). Finally, the prophets announce that Israel's time is up.

"An adversary shall surround the land and bring down your defenses from you, and your strongholds shall be plundered," the prophet Amos predicts with bitter irony to a materially prosperous but morally bankrupt people. "Thus says the LORD: 'As the shepherd rescues from the mouth of the lion two legs, or a piece of an ear, so shall the people of Israel who dwell in Samaria be rescued'" (Amos 3:11–12).

Israel's prosperity eventually turns to want. The hard-pressed people of the Northern Kingdom begin to chafe under oppression from Assyria, a rising military superpower, and start to plot rebellion, but without the Lord's blessing. God is using the cruel Assyrians to execute his judgment.

"They shall not remain in the land of the LORD," another prophet, Hosea, announces, "but . . . shall return to Egypt, and they shall eat unclean food in Assyria" (Hosea 9:3).

Eventually, Israel, heedless of the warnings of the prophets, rebels against its overlords. The brutal empire responds by besieging and destroying the capital and many other Israelite cities. Then Emperor Sargon II deports tens of thousands of upper-class Israelites, replacing them with peoples from other vassal states. The resulting mixture of Israelites with foreign populations will produce the despised Samaritans, who institute a false religious system that mocks temple worship in Jerusalem.[1]

Israel rejects its calling to bless the nations and, as prophesied, ends up among them as captives, never to return.

APPLICATION

It's not how you begin; it's how you finish.

7

Judgment against Jerusalem and the Babylonian Captivity

Jeremiah 25:8–11; Amos 2:4–5

Whoever its king, Jerusalem is the locus of the divine program. As such, the people expect the Southern Kingdom to endure, come what may in the north—or, indeed, in the rest of the world. They sing:

> There is a river whose streams make glad the city of God,
>   the holy habitation of the Most High.
> God is in the midst of her; she shall not be moved; . . .
> The LORD of hosts is with us;
>   the God of Jacob is our fortress.
>
> Psalm 46:4–5, 7

And for a time the tiny kingdom of Judah, in a very dangerous neighborhood, manages not only to survive but to prosper. Miraculously God turns back Assyria, which has already swallowed up the Northern Kingdom. The nation enjoys the rules of Josiah, Hezekiah, and other spiritual stalwarts.

Yet even the holy habitation cannot resist the downward pull of human depravity and demonic attack. Of Judah's twenty kings, only eight can be considered "good monarchs."[1] Finally, the nation, like the Northern Kingdom, succumbs to the idol worship that has stalked God's people since the time of Moses.

However, as a new superpower, Babylon, mounts the world stage, God continues to send his prophets. Their agenda is not to satisfy the intellectual curiosity of their hearers about the future, but to pull them back from the brink of disaster. When the people stop their ears, they seal their own fate. So Amos pronounces the heretofore unimaginable judgment: "I will send a fire upon Judah, and it shall devour the strongholds of Jerusalem" (see Amos 2:4–5).

The city will be consumed with fire, the stronghold overthrown. The prophet Jeremiah makes a series of bleak pronouncements about what is coming.

> I will send for all the tribes of the north, declares the LORD, and for Nebuchadnezzar the king of Babylon, my servant, and I will bring them against this land and its inhabitants, and against all these surrounding nations. I will devote them to destruction, and make them a horror, a hissing, and an everlasting desolation. . . . This whole land shall become a ruin and a waste, and these nations shall serve the king of Babylon seventy years.
>
> Jeremiah 25:8–9, 11

Not only will Judah be destroyed; its people will be carried off with their pagan neighbors by Nebuchadnezzar, who in this fearsome task is called the Lord's servant. The Jewish people will stay in Babylon for seventy years, while the land is laid waste.

Then, under wicked King Zedekiah, the national calamity happens, right on schedule.

> And in the ninth year of his reign, in the tenth month, on the tenth day of the month, Nebuchadnezzar king of Babylon came with all his army against Jerusalem and laid siege to it. . . . Then they captured the king and brought him up to the king of Babylon at Riblah, and they passed sentence on him. They slaughtered the sons of Zedekiah before his eyes, and put out the eyes of Zedekiah and bound him in chains and took him to Babylon. . . .
>
> And all the army of the Chaldeans, who were with the captain of the guard, broke down the walls around Jerusalem. And the rest of the people who were left in the city and the deserters who had deserted to the king of Babylon, together with the rest of the multitude, Nebuzaradan the captain of the guard carried into exile.
>
> 2 Kings 25:1, 6–7, 10–11

The people of God, blessed to be a global blessing, go into seventy years of exile. Is the Lord's plan for the world over?

APPLICATION

With great privilege comes great responsibility.

8

The Seventy Weeks

Daniel 9:24–27

Where do you go after the worst thing that could possibly happen *happens*? For Daniel the prophet, you go to Scripture and to prayer. Jerusalem and the temple have been destroyed, the people exiled from the land of promise by Nebuchadnezzar. God's plan of salvation seemingly is dead. But a now ancient Daniel, deported to Babylon as a young man, has been reading Scripture—the book of Jeremiah to be exact.

"This whole land shall become a ruin and a waste, and these nations shall serve the king of Babylon seventy years," Jeremiah's prophecy predicts. "Then after seventy years are completed, I will punish the king of Babylon and that nation, the land of the Chaldeans, for their iniquity, declares the Lord, making the land an everlasting waste" (Jer. 25:11–12).

In fulfillment of this prophecy, in 605 BC, Nebuchadnezzar came to Jerusalem and carried off Daniel and other future leaders, wiping out Jerusalem in 586 BC. In response to the prophecy, Daniel confesses the people's sin. You can read this amazing confession in Daniel 9:4–16, followed by his plea for national deliverance in verses 17–19.

And indeed, against the trend of world history, the captive Jewish people are soon released. In 539 BC—seventy years, according to the Jewish calendar, after the deportation—Babylon falls to Cyrus and the Persians, and the door is opened to a return to the Promised Land. The prophecy has been fulfilled. God reigns.

Yet the Lord's work is not finished. In response to his prophet's prayer, God sends the angel Gabriel with a message about the future, beyond the return from exile. The prophecy of the "seventy sevens" or "seventy weeks" has alternately intrigued, confused, and thrilled God's followers.

Seventy weeks are decreed about your people and your holy city, to finish the transgression, to put an end to sin, and to atone for iniquity, to bring in everlasting righteousness, to seal both vision and prophet, and to anoint a most holy place. Know therefore and understand that from the going out of the word to restore and build Jerusalem to the coming of an anointed one, a prince, there shall be seven weeks. Then for sixty-two weeks it shall be built again with squares and moat, but in a troubled time. And after the sixty-two weeks, an anointed one shall be cut off and shall have nothing. And the people of the prince who is to come shall destroy the city and the sanctuary. Its end shall come with a flood, and to the end there shall be war. Desolations are decreed. And he shall make a strong covenant with many for one week, and for half of the week he shall put an end to sacrifice and offering. And on the wing of abominations shall come one who makes desolate, until the decreed end is poured out on the desolator.

Daniel 9:24–27

The prophecy divides the seventy sevens into three distinct periods: seven weeks, sixty-two weeks, and one week. Commentators differ about whether the weeks are literal years, whether there are gaps between these periods, and what the various events signify. Keeping in mind that Christ is the ultimate goal of prophecy, here is one interpretation that makes a lot of sense (remembering that some prophecies are made clear only in hindsight).

The 70 sevens are 490 years that followed "the word to restore and build Jerusalem." This word likely occurred in 458 BC (see Ezra 7:1–7), under King Artaxerxes of Persia. So 490 years from 458 BC is AD 33, when many scholars believe Christ, the "anointed one . . . cut off," was crucified. This fits well with the stated end of the prophecy, which is "to finish the transgression, to put an end to sin, and to atone for iniquity, to bring in everlasting righteousness, to seal both vision and prophet, and to anoint a most holy place." The death and resurrection of Christ atoned for sin and made possible everlasting righteousness through faith.

Some scholars say the final week is yet to come—when a coming Antichrist rules the earth for a seven-year period of tribulation before God defeats him. Many see Gabriel's mention of abominations as occurring several times, first during the reign of Antiochus IV Epiphanes, who desecrated the rebuilt temple with an altar to Zeus while ruling the Seleucid Empire in 167 BC. Jesus told his disciples that the prophecy would be further fulfilled when the Romans destroyed Herod's temple in AD 70 and in the last days.[1] God is patient in working his will, and many prophecies have several stages of fulfillment.

It seems abundantly clear that the prophecy finds its ultimate fulfillment in Christ hundreds—and now thousands—of years in the future. The prophecy's many details are worked out precisely according to God's specific timetable, even if some still seem blurry to us. God is in control of history. For people who have experienced the worst that life has to offer, this is good news indeed.

APPLICATION

**For God's people, misery always has
an expiration date.**

9

Return via Cyrus

Isaiah 44:24, 28; 45:1–6

The prophet Isaiah, the son of Amoz, ministered during a time of national upheaval in tiny Judah. Israel, the Northern Kingdom, has just been obliterated by the cruel Assyrian empire, which continues to exact tribute from Judah. Judah's king, Hezekiah, also chooses to revolt, and King Sennacherib of Assyria, like a bird of prey, swoops down south and west for the kill. The Lord, however, turns him back (see Isaiah 36–37).

Yet Isaiah, like other prophets, predicts that ultimately the Jews will fail and face exile in Babylon (see Isa. 39:5–7). But he sees beyond this coming disaster to a bright hope—that God's people will one day return to the Promised Land. Further, God even tells Isaiah the name of the one who will deliver the people from exile: *Cyrus*.

> I am the LORD, . . .
> who says of Cyrus, "He is my shepherd,
>   and he shall fulfill all my purpose";
> saying of Jerusalem, "She shall be built,"
>   and of the temple, "Your foundation shall be laid."
>
> Isaish 44:24, 28

Then God explains why he is using Cyrus:

> Thus says the LORD to his anointed, to Cyrus,
>   whose right hand I have grasped,

to subdue nations before him . . .
> "I will give you the treasures of darkness
>   and the hoards in secret places,
> that you may know that it is I, the LORD,
>   the God of Israel, who call you by your name.
> For the sake of my servant Jacob,
>   and Israel my chosen,
> I call you by your name,
>   I name you, though you do not know me. . . .
>   I equip you, though you do not know me,
> that people may know, from the rising of the sun
>   and from the west, that there is none besides me;
> I am the LORD, and there is no other."

Isaiah 45:1–6

As predicted, Jerusalem fell in 586 BC to the Babylonians, and the people were exiled. A leader named Cyrus began ruling Persia in 559 BC. This Cyrus took Babylon in 539 BC without violence, ending its superpower status. A famous archaeological find, the Cyrus Cylinder, in words eerily similar to Isaiah's, said the new ruler conquered the fabled city at the instigation of its patron deity: "Marduk . . . sought a righteous prince, after his own heart, whom he took by the hand. Cyrus . . . he called by name, to lordship over the whole world he appointed him."[1]

Cyrus had an enlightened policy toward captive peoples. "When he conquered an area or a city," John Currid and David Barrett note, "there were no general massacres, no deportations, and no desecrations of local shrines. In fact, the Persian policy was to encourage local customs and cults."[2]

Cyrus did the same with the Jewish exiles, encouraging them to return and rebuild the temple. Ezra the scribe describes what happened: "In the first year of Cyrus king of Persia, that the word of the LORD by the mouth of Jeremiah might be fulfilled,[3] the LORD stirred up the spirit of Cyrus king of Persia, so that he made a proclamation throughout all his kingdom and also put it in writing" (Ezra 1:1).

The proclamation, like the Cyrus Cylinder with Marduk, credits the "local deity" (God) with inspiring Cyrus to call the Jews to return and rebuild. "Thus says Cyrus king of Persia: The LORD, the God of heaven, has given me all the kingdoms of the earth, and he has charged me to build him a house at Jerusalem, which is in Judah" (v. 2).

This description, however, seems to hint that ultimately Cyrus may have had more than a mere political use for the Lord. But even if Cyrus did not know the God of Israel, it is clear that the Lord knew *him*.

APPLICATION

**Whatever occurs among the nations, God's people
can rest in the sovereignty of a loving Lord.**

10

The New Covenant

Jeremiah 31:31–33

Judaism is commonly known as a religion of law. Indeed, there are 613 commandments, or *mitzvoth*, in the Hebrew Scriptures,[1] what Christians refer to as the Old Testament. Today when a Jewish boy turns thirteen, his family and community hold a *bar mitzvah* ceremony, a rite of passage recognizing him as a "son of commandment."

In the Old Testament, however, the Jewish people ultimately failed to live according to God's law and were carried into exile, their central role in God's plan of salvation *seemingly* over. In the centuries before Jesus, however, the Jewish people resolved as never before to follow the law and so prompt God to bless them once again.

Under Cyrus, the temple was rebuilt, but those who had been around to see Solomon's temple wept when they saw the new, much smaller version (see Ezra 3:1–13). The people wondered why their newfound obedience was so little rewarded. The gloom continued as they remained under the thumb of the Greek and then the Roman empires. Why was the kingdom of God not reinstated? What were they missing?

The Old Testament prophets, of course, recognized that mere outward adherence to the law was insufficient. Religious observance, divorced from a transformed heart, is worse than useless; it is damning. "I hate, I despise your feasts, and I take no delight in your solemn assemblies," the prophet Amos thundered for God. "Even though you offer me your burnt offerings and grain offerings, I will not accept them; and the peace offerings of your fattened animals, I will not look upon them" (Amos 5:21–22).

The Lord declared that following him requires more than brute obedience. The indictment: "This people draw near with their mouth and honor me with their lips, while their hearts are far from me" (Isa. 29:13).

Still, through the centuries many Jews held to the conceit that life with God was a simple matter of obedience. In Matthew 19 a rich young man in the first century asked a rabbi named Jesus what one must do to receive eternal life, and the answer was straightforward: "If you would enter life, keep the commandments" (v. 17). Suddenly the impossibility of obeying all 613 *mitzvoth* must have dawned on him, because he quickly asked a desperate follow-up question: "*Which ones?*" Apparently he was hoping for an escape clause. *No one* could obey every jot and tittle of the law!

The rich young man apparently needed to reread Jeremiah.

> Behold, the days are coming, declares the LORD, when I will make a new covenant with the house of Israel and the house of Judah, not like the covenant that I made with their fathers on the day when I took them by the hand to bring them out of the land of Egypt, my covenant that they broke, though I was their husband, declares the LORD. For this is the covenant that I will make with the house of Israel after those days, declares the LORD: I will put my law within them, and I will write it on their hearts. And I will be their God, and they shall be my people.
>
> Jeremiah 31:31–33

It was time for a new spiritual approach. Because people were unable to keep the old sacrificial system, Jesus announced that he was instituting a "new covenant" with his blood (Luke 22:20). This new understanding between God and man would be based not on futile attempts to follow the letter of the law, but on being led by the Holy Spirit, because "the letter kills, but the Spirit gives life" (2 Cor. 3:6).

The old approach revealed the people's *guilt* before a holy God; the new, prophesied by Jeremiah and inaugurated by Jesus, proclaimed God's *grace*: "For the law was given through Moses; grace and truth came through Jesus Christ" (John 1:17). What God required of his people, God would graciously supply.

APPLICATION

**God looks at our heart, not merely
our outward acts.**

11

All Israel Will Be Saved

Romans 11:12–29

The apostle Paul was called to spread the word about the Good News "to the Jew first and also to the Greek" (Rom. 1:16). As a brilliant disciple of the great rabbi Gamaliel, Paul should have been able to expect a warm welcome from his fellow Jews in Jerusalem and in the rest of the Roman Empire. That's because prophets in the Hebrew Scriptures had already predicted the New Covenant (see previous chapter). Further, Isaiah had prophesied that the Jewish people would turn to their Redeemer *en masse*:

> "And a Redeemer will come to Zion,
>   to those in Jacob who turn from transgression," declares the LORD.

> "And as for me, this is my covenant with them," says the LORD: "My Spirit that is upon you, and my words that I have put in your mouth, shall not depart out of your mouth, or out of the mouth of your offspring, or out of the mouth of your children's offspring," says the LORD, "from this time forth and forevermore."

> Isaiah 59:20–21

And yet Paul's reception from his fellow Jews was anything but warm. Three times he received the Jewish punishment of forty lashes minus one. Another time he escaped his enraged countrymen by being lowered in a basket from the Damascus city wall. Everywhere he went, most Jews rejected the Jewish Messiah, while many Gentiles received him.

The paradox was breaking Paul's passionate heart. As he exclaimed, "I have great sorrow and unceasing anguish in my heart. . . . for the sake of my brothers, my kinsmen according to the flesh" (Rom. 9:2–3).

But Paul knew his Hebrew Scriptures, and he believed that a greater harvest of Jewish souls was coming. Confidently he prophesied to a mixed congregation of Jews and Gentiles in Rome:

> Lest you be wise in your own sight, I do not want you to be unaware of this mystery, brothers: a partial hardening has come upon Israel, until the fullness of the Gentiles has come in. And in this way all Israel will be saved. . . .
>
> As regards the gospel, they are enemies for your sake. But as regards election, they are beloved for the sake of their forefathers. For the gifts and the calling of God are irrevocable.
>
> Romans 11:25–29

Paul knew that God, who had called the Jewish people in the first place, would never give up on them. *They* had failed him repeatedly (in Abraham, in the wilderness, in both the Northern and Southern Kingdoms, and in the Jewish leaders' rejection of Jesus), but God would never fail *them*.

In fact the widespread (but not complete) rejection of Jesus by the Jewish leaders of Paul's day opened the door to the huge ingathering of non-Jews, the apostle said. Of course, Jews have believed in Jesus as their long expected Messiah from the beginning (all of Christ's apostles were Jews). One day many more Jewish people will join them, fully experiencing the blessing of Abraham so they can in turn bless the world. "Now if their trespass means riches for the world, and if their failure means riches for the Gentiles, how much more will their full inclusion mean! . . . For if their rejection means the reconciliation of the world, what will their acceptance mean but life from the dead?" (vv. 12, 15).

It is a prophecy worth waiting for—and working toward.

APPLICATION

**God will never abandon the Jewish people,
and neither should we.**

The Nations

12

Famine in Egypt

Genesis 41:25–32

In movies such as *The Ten Commandments* or *Prince of Egypt*, it is easy to see the Egyptians as the bad guys. They were oppressing God's people and got what they deserved—good riddance! The only thing is, the biblical picture is much more complex. Consider the Old Testament story of Joseph.

Egypt, while undoubtedly polytheistic, in a very real sense was the means of salvation for Joseph. His jealous brothers had sold him into slavery. Then Joseph was framed by a high-ranking official's wife whose advances he had spurned. Joseph was imprisoned and apparently forgotten, but word eventually spread about his ability to interpret dreams.

The news made it all the way to Pharaoh, who was troubled by a frightening vision of seven lean cows devouring seven fat cows, followed by seven bad ears of grain replacing seven good ones. None of his pagan advisers had a clue, so Egypt's sovereign sent for Joseph, the dream-revealer.

> Joseph said to Pharaoh, "The dreams of Pharaoh are one; God has revealed to Pharaoh what he is about to do. . . . There will come seven years of great plenty throughout all the land of Egypt, but after them there will arise seven years of famine, and all the plenty will be forgotten in the land of Egypt. . . . for it will be very severe. And the doubling of Pharaoh's dream means that the thing is fixed by God, and God will shortly bring it about."
>
> Genesis 41:25, 29, 31–32

Then Joseph moves from the prophecy to a practical solution. Pharaoh ought to appoint a man with wisdom to oversee the national stockpiling of grain during the seven good years, for distribution during the seven lean. Pharaoh, stunned by the specificity of Joseph's prophecy and the good sense of his plan, chooses *him*.

And, just as predicted, seven years of abundance come, during which Joseph makes sure the nation saves its abundance, followed by seven years of famine. The crisis is so severe that his father, Jacob, and Joseph's despicable brothers must leave the Promised Land and trek to the land of the Nile to buy food. Graciously Joseph forgives them, saves them, and is God's instrument in allowing the people of Israel to live safely in Egypt for generations until the coming of Moses. But Israel's salvation is only part of the Egypt story.

When Jacob dies, Joseph's brothers fear that Egypt's second-in-command might finally choose to exact revenge for the abuse they had dished out so many years before. But Joseph has God's perspective on the incident—a global perspective.

"Do not fear, for am I in the place of God?" he assures them. "As for you, you meant evil against me, but God meant it for good, to bring it about that many people should be kept alive, as they are today" (50:19–20). Yes, the "many people . . . kept alive" included the Jewish people but they also included the Egyptian people and any other peoples who came to Egypt during the famine.

Joseph's prophecy was meant not just for Israel but for the world. And in fact it illustrates how Abraham, the father of the Jewish people, was blessed to be a blessing.

APPLICATION

**God cares for the whole world,
and so should we.**

13

Nineveh

Threatened and Spared

Jonah 3:1–4

In the middle of the ninth century BC, the cruel Assyrian monarch Shalmaneser III defeated a coalition of kings that included Ahab of Israel. Shalmaneser III "claimed an overwhelming triumph in which [the Assyrian king] made the blood of his enemies flow down the valleys and scattered their corpses far and wide."[1]

The famous Black Obelisk depicts the Israelite King Jehu kneeling before the pagan king, paying a tribute of gold, silver, and other costly tokens of the Northern Kingdom's humiliation. Shalmaneser III called himself "the mighty king, king of the universe, the king without a rival, the autocrat, the powerful one of the four regions of the world, who shatters the might of the princes of the whole world, who has smashed all of his foes like pots."[2] Such blasphemous boasting would sting like a slap in the face to followers of the true King of the universe.

About a century later, however, Assyria is in decline, and little Israel, under the evil but prosperous Jeroboam II, has taken advantage of the power vacuum. Yet the Northern Kingdom and Jonah the prophet have not forgotten the terrors the Assyrians inflicted. Neither have they forgiven.

So God sends Jonah with a message to Nineveh, an ancient city about five hundred miles northeast of Israel, in the heart of the Assyrian empire.

The Lord's directions are clear: "Arise, go to Nineveh, that great city, and call out against it, for their evil has come up before me" (Jon. 1:2).

Instead, Jonah, living out one of the best-known stories in the Bible, flees in the opposite direction. But using a terrible storm and a great fish, God brings his recalcitrant prophet back to his task—warning Nineveh of coming judgment:

> Then the word of the LORD came to Jonah the second time, saying, "Arise, go to Nineveh, that great city, and call out against it the message that I tell you." So Jonah arose and went to Nineveh, according to the word of the LORD. . . . And he called out, "Yet forty days, and Nineveh shall be overthrown!"
>
> Jonah 3:1–4

The response of the Assyrian people is immediate—not scorn or persecution but repentance. The evil Ninevites, from the king on down, turn to prayer and fasting. They are hoping against hope that God might change his mind. "Who knows?" the king says helplessly. "God may turn and relent and turn from his fierce anger, so that we may not perish" (v. 9). And indeed the Lord *does* relent (v. 10).

However, Jonah, a confirmed hater of the Assyrians, is neither amused nor surprised. When the predicted disaster does not come, Jonah's prayer is almost an accusation: "I knew that you are a gracious God and merciful, slow to anger and abounding in steadfast love, and relenting from disaster. Therefore now, O LORD, please take my life from me, for it is better for me to die than to live" (4:2–3).

An unforgiving Jonah knows that God's seemingly absolute message of judgment depends on the response of its recipients. And in fact we all stand before God, responsible for whatever light we have received: "The men of Nineveh will rise up at the judgment with this generation and condemn it," Jesus said, "for they repented at the preaching of Jonah, and behold, something greater than Jonah is here" (Matt. 12:41).

APPLICATION

**We ALL must repent, and God will forgive
anyone who does.**

14

Syria

End of a Civilization

Amos 1:3–5

Syria,[1] or the land of the Arameans, has a long history in the Bible. The Arameans make their first appearance on the world stage in the Table of Nations of Genesis 10. Like the Jewish people, they are sons of Shem.

Genesis 22:20–21 identifies Aram as a descendent of Nahor, who was one of Abram's brothers in Haran. When Jacob, Abram's grandson, was forced to flee the Promised Land, he went to Laban, his uncle, in Haran. When Jacob finally left Haran, he and Laban set up a stone monument that was called *Galeed* (Gilead). Syria and Israel were related by both blood and treaty. Israelites who brought their firstfruits to God were to confess, "My father was a wandering Aramean" (Deut. 26:5).[2]

Yet by the time of Solomon, the small but vigorous kingdom of Aram-damascus was a constant thorn in the side of the Jewish people. The Arameans, led by thuggish kings such as Ben-hadad, would periodically attack Israel or Judah. All sense of brotherly concern had long since evaporated.

But when the brutal Shalmaneser III of Assyria came onto the scene, Israel and Syria allied against their common foe. By God's grace they were given a reprieve—but foolishly turned on each other. When the alliance fell apart, Shalmaneser III returned and devastated Aramean territory and exacted tribute from the Jews. During this time of instability (before 805 BC), the Arameans took advantage and committed "many atrocities" in the bordering region of Gilead.[3]

Then sometime after 793 BC, Amos, a shepherd from the small Judean city of Tekoa, steps forward with a message of judgment:

> For three transgressions of Damascus,
>   and for four, I will not revoke the punishment,
> because they have threshed Gilead
>   with threshing sledges of iron.
> So I will send a fire upon the house of Hazael,
>   and it shall devour the strongholds of Ben-hadad.
>   . . . and the people of Syria shall go into exile to Kir.
>
> Amos 1:3–5

Though Assyria remains the greater long-term threat to the people of God, Amos zeroes in on the local cutthroats in Damascus. They have "threshed Gilead" with iron. Threshing is an ancient agricultural practice in which grain is separated from the husks with a heavy wooden sledge. Pitiless Syria, however, has used iron.[4]

Though Gilead is the place of a significant treaty between Israel and Aram, Aram has "treated the people of Gilead as though they were nothing but a pile of grain, crushing them into the ground."[5] Kir represents the ancestral homeland of the Arameans. Still, we see God's grace with Syria in the account of Naaman's healing and conversion to following the one true God (2 Kings 5).

Judgment comes swiftly in 735 BC. Rezin, an Aramean vassal under Assyria, has annexed large swaths of Jewish territory east of the Jordan; his troops are now besieging Jerusalem. Ahaz, the king of Judah, sends a bribe to Tiglath-pileser, the new ruler of Assyria.

Tiglath-pileser comes to his aid—with a vengeance. Assyria's modus operandi is "a ruthless deportation of peoples in order to prevent future rebellions"[6]—at least those who survive are deported. Second Kings 16:9 reports, "The king of Assyria marched up against Damascus and took it, carrying its people captive to Kir, and he killed Rezin." They were being sent unceremoniously back to their place of origin. The proud civilization of ancient Syria, for all intents and purposes, was at an end.

APPLICATION

**Your pedigree or family history will not
protect you in the day of judgment.**

15

Tyre's Watery Doom

Isaiah 23:1; Ezekiel 26:2–6

The Phoenicians were one of the true wonders of the ancient world. Situated on a parcel on the Mediterranean coast that was a mere 160 miles long and just 20 miles wide, this people distinguished themselves in a rough neighborhood. Phoenicians in the city of Byblos developed a syllabic alphabet that was precursor to several alphabetic scripts, including Greek, Aramaic, Etruscan, Latin, Arabic, and eventually English. From Byblos we get the English word *Bible*.

Great traders, they were also noted for extraordinary seafaring skill, necessary because of their small territory. Their two greatest cities were Sidon, on the coast, and the island stronghold of Tyre, which was thought to be impregnable.

One source notes, "They became the most skillful shipbuilders and navigators of their time. They worked the silver mines of Spain, passed through the Strait of Gibraltar, and founded the city of Cadiz on the southern coast of Spain. They sailed to the British Isles for tin and may have ventured around southern Africa."[1] Tyrian purple was an expensive dye made from the crushed shells of mussels.

The Phoenicians, like the Jews, were a Semitic people. But unlike official Israel, they worshiped the detestable gods Astarte, Moloch (also Molech), and Baal. However, Tyre, and its king, Hiram, supplied cedar and workmen to both David and Solomon. Yet the comity would not last.

In the waning days of the Southern Kingdom, Nebuchadnezzar, king of Babylon, is on the move. While he will eventually mete out disaster on God's people, the prophets see his bloody reign as God's judgment on many of the surrounding pagan nations too (see Jer. 27:6).

Isaiah, who wrote from Judah during the fall of the Northern Kingdom, foresees the collapse of Tyre from afar: "Wail, O ships of Tarshish, for Tyre is laid waste, without house or harbor!" (Isa. 23:1).

The later prophet Ezekiel, writing between 592 and 570 BC, spells out what will happen to Tyre, which rejoiced at Jerusalem's fall:

> Son of man, because Tyre said concerning Jerusalem, "Aha, the gate of the peoples is broken; it has swung open to me. I shall be replenished, now that she is laid waste," therefore thus says the Lord God: Behold, I am against you, O Tyre, and will bring up many nations against you, as the sea brings up its waves. They shall destroy the walls of Tyre and break down her towers, and I will scrape her soil from her and make her a bare rock. She shall be in the midst of the sea a place for the spreading of nets, for I have spoken, declares the Lord God. And she shall become plunder for the nations, and her daughters on the mainland shall be killed by the sword. Then they will know that I am the Lord.
>
> Ezekiel 26:2–6

According to the later Jewish historian Josephus, Nebuchadnezzar, with soldiers from many lands, laid siege to Tyre for thirteen years, starting in 586 BC, the same year Jerusalem fell. While Nebuchadnezzar wreaked havoc on the mainland, Tyre survived. So was the prophecy nullified? Not at all.

In 332 BC another fearsome world leader, Alexander the Great, built a massive causeway of rubble from the mainland to the island. His multinational force crossed over—in a sense like the Israelites through the Red Sea, on dry land—and laid waste to Tyre. The once proud city was scraped down to its rocky foundation, a place where fishermen spread their nets. Another prophecy fulfilled.

APPLICATION

**God's arrows of justice may tarry but they
always find their mark.**

16

Nineveh's Judgment

Nahum 1:7–8; 2:1–9

Assyria was the world's first military dictatorship, "an entity devoted exclusively to war and conquest."[1] Around 1,000 BC the Assyrians created a standing army of thirty thousand men and funded a continual program of weapons development. The Assyrians developed the feared *heliopolis*, a 100-foot-high siege tower that "terrorized the Near East for a century."

Ernest Volkman writes, "Once inside a besieged city, the Assyrians showed no mercy; like all succeeding military dictatorships, they believed in the use of terror as a weapon. The entire population of a captured city was slain or mutilated; word of their fate was spread far and wide by Assyrian messengers as a warning."

Inside the fortified royal city of Nineveh, however, life was considerably more refined.[2] The city "contained such luxuries as public squares, parks, botanical gardens, and even a zoo." Nineveh was protected by thick walls. The Khosr River flowed under two of them, across the city, and into the famous Tigris River situated just to the west.

Assyria conquered Israel, the Northern Kingdom, and its walled city of Samaria, deporting the Jewish population in 722 BC. Such brutality was especially appalling, given that the Lord spared Nineveh under the ministry of the prophet Jonah, which had ended mere decades before. The Lord noticed, replacing Jonah's contingent prophecy of warning with an unequivocal and detailed pronouncement of the great city's doom. This came about a century later from the prophet Nahum, who probably wrote between 660 and 630 BC:[3]

> The LORD is good,
>   a stronghold in the day of trouble;
> he knows those who take refuge in him.
>   But with an overflowing flood
> he will make a complete end of the adversaries,
>   and will pursue his enemies into darkness.
>
> Nahum 1:7–8

Later Nahum expands on this deadly vision, proclaiming a coming attack:

> The scatterer has come up against you.
>   Man the ramparts;
>   watch the road;
> dress for battle;
>   collect all your strength. . . .
> The chariots race madly through the streets;
>   they rush to and fro through the squares. . . .
> they hasten to the wall;
>   the siege tower is set up.
> The river gates are opened;
>   the palace melts away; . . .
> Nineveh is like a pool
>   whose waters run away.
> "Halt! Halt!" they cry,
>   but none turns back.
> Plunder the silver,
>   plunder the gold!
> There is no end of the treasure
>   or of the wealth of all precious things.
>
> Nahum 2:1, 4–9

Nahum expands on the image of water, saying that the city's river gates will be breached. He sees a siege tower, but this one is not of Assyrian make. The city is in utter panic and then it is taken. Such a vision would seem like utter nonsense to Nahum's contemporaries, who trembled at the mere mention of Assyria.

Historians, however, tell us about the remarkable fall of the mighty metropolis in 612 BC. The Babylonians and the Medes, two rising powers, marched on Nineveh. Conventional means of attack were futile, so their armies dammed the rivers that flowed into the city. The pent-up water was suddenly released, smashing through one of the outer walls. The invaders then looted Nineveh, leaving only "heaps of debris."[4]

The brutal Assyrian empire, which had once repented, was now overwhelmed, never again to see the light of day.

APPLICATION

**God's past mercies will not save us
if we reject him today.**

17

Edom Brought Low

Obadiah 3–4

Israel well understood fraternal strife, which was woven into its very DNA as a people. When Rebekah, who was the patriarch Isaac's wife, became pregnant, the twins in her womb struggled against each other. The Lord told her that they were actually two nations, and that the older—against all cultural norms—would serve the younger. On the day they were born, Esau, all red and hairy, emerged first. Yet the second, Jacob, had a firm grasp of his brother's heel. It was a portent of the deception and hatred that would come to dominate their relationship in the decades to come.[1]

By the time of Moses and the exodus of God's chosen people from Egypt, the disunity between the descendents of Jacob (Israel) and Esau (Edom) has hardened like Edom's red sandstone cliffs. When Moses leads his people back to the land of promise from Egypt, he seeks safe passage through the land of Edom, which is south and east of the Dead Sea.

The answer from Edom's king is swift and decisive: "You shall not pass through, lest I come out with the sword against you" (Num. 20:18; see vv. 14–21). So, rejected by their brothers, the Israelites are forced to take the long way around.

Later when Jerusalem fell to Babylon in 586 BC, not only did the Edomites gloat, they joined in the looting, "handed over captives to Babylon, and possessed lands in the Negeb area to the south."[2] Today we might call such treachery "piling on." God called it the end of the line for Edom. "Thus says the LORD," prophesied Amos:

> For three transgressions of Edom,
>   and for four, I will not revoke the punishment,
> because he pursued his brother with the sword
>   and cast off all pity,
> and his anger tore perpetually,
>   and he kept his wrath forever.
> So I will send a fire upon Teman,
>   and it shall devour the strongholds of Bozrah.
>
> Amos 1:11–12

Yet the Edomites felt secure in their mountain strongholds, which were "practically impregnable from the assault of enemies."[3] The prophet Obadiah accurately reported their mood, and the Lord's righteous response:

> The pride of your heart has deceived you,
>   you who live in the clefts of the rock,
>   in your lofty dwelling,
> who say in your heart,
>   "Who will bring me down to the ground?"
> Though you soar aloft like the eagle,
>   though your nest is set among the stars,
>   from there I will bring you down.
>
> Obadiah 3–4

Edom's doom is sure, it represents a larger truth, and it is fair, Obadiah says: "For the day of the LORD is near upon all the nations. As you have done, it shall be done to you; your deeds shall return on your own head" (v. 15).

For a while, at least, the prophecy goes unfulfilled. Quickly, neighboring states Ammon and Moab come under Babylon's domination, but not Edom. Then in 553 BC Nabonidus, the last king of Babylon, annexes Edom, "leaving a carving on a remote cliff not far from the capital Bozrah . . . to mark his triumph. Signs of destruction by fire from that time have been found in some Edomite towns, and . . . the kingdom of Edom ended."[4]

APPLICATION

Bearing a grudge is ultimately self-destructive.

18

Philistia
Drowning in Judgment

Isaiah 14:31; Jeremiah 47:2; Amos 1:7–8

Egypt is recovering from the painful loss of its Jewish slaves and a round of devastating plagues from the hand of God. Soon the ancient colossus of the Near East faces a new problem. Perhaps sensing weakness, just after 1200 BC, a mysterious coalition called the Sea Peoples launches a land and sea invasion of its southern neighbor. In desperation, Egypt turns back the invaders, using archers, its massive navy, and brutal hand-to-hand combat. Among the losers are the Peleset, or Peleste, who are forced to settle along the southern Mediterranean coast. They are the Philistines, from whom we get the name Palestine, the modern name for the entire region.[1]

Unlike other powers in the region, the Philistines have no king or centralized state. Instead, analogous to the Greeks of this era, they are clustered in city-states: Gaza, Ashkelon, Ashdod, Gath, and Ekron. Whether singly or in concert, these Philistine city-states will constitute a major thorn in Israel's side for much of its history.

In the days before Israel had a king, the Philistines subjugated the Jews. The Israelite army of Saul trembled before one Goliath of Gath before a certain shepherd boy named David fired a single stone into the pagan giant's forehead. Other Jewish kings who battled the Philistines included Uzziah and Hezekiah.

The Philistines, who (according to Deut. 2:23; Jer. 47:4; and Amos 9:7) originally migrated from Caphtor (possibly Crete or on the southern coast of Asia Minor),[2] soon enough adopt the Caananite deities of their surroundings. Among these gods is Dagon, for whom temples are constructed in Gaza and Ashdod. Residents of Ekron worship a deity called Baal-zebub, which later comes to be referred to as Satan (Mark 3:22).

Though a small group on the global stage, the Philistines, because of their near constant opposition to God's people, are the withering objects of prophecy. Isaiah prophesies in 714 BC:

> Wail, O gate; cry out, O city;
>   melt in fear, O Philistia, all of you!
> For smoke comes out of the north,
>   and there is no straggler in his ranks
>   Isaiah 14:31

The Lord also predicts through Amos:

> I will send a fire upon the wall of Gaza,
>   and it shall devour her strongholds.
> I will cut off the inhabitants from Ashdod,
>   and him who holds the scepter from Ashkelon;
> I will turn my hand against Ekron,
>   and the remnant of the Philistines shall perish.
>   Amos 1:7–8

Yet for a century the Philistines continue to oppress God's people, heedless of the warnings. As the time of God's judgment nears, Jeremiah also predicts the destruction of Philistia from the north, saying,

> Thus says the LORD:
> Behold, waters are rising out of the north,
>   and shall become an overflowing torrent;
> they shall overflow the land and all that fills it,
>   the city and those who dwell in it
>   Jeremiah 47:2

Finally, in 604 BC, the predicted destruction comes. Babylon pours in like a flaming torrent against Ashkelon, leaving the city smoldering; archaeologists have discovered a male in the ruins with a smashed skull.[3]

The Philistine era is soon over, and Israel's perpetual enemies disappear "from the pages of the Bible and from secular history."[4]

APPLICATION

**Those who resist God's blessings
should fear God's curses.**

19

Ammon

Actions and Attitudes

Ezekiel 25:6–7; Amos 1:13–15

In the time of the patriarchs, the land could not accommodate all the flocks, herds, and servants of Abraham and his nephew, Lot. So faithful Abraham, it seems, put the entire plan of salvation on the line, offering Lot whatever territory he chose—even the Promised Land. Lot, however, chose the more fertile east. The disastrous account of his forced departure from the wicked city of Sodom is well-known. Later the cave-dwelling Lot had relations with his daughters (Genesis 19). One bore the founder of the Moabites; the other bore Ben-Ammi, founder of the Ammonites.

The Ammonites, with their citadel capital of Rabbath-Ammon (modern-day Amman, Jordan), inhabited the Transjordan, abutting Jewish territory. Conflicts between Israel and Ammon were inevitable, and frequent.[1] The sons of Ben-Ammi, like the sons of Esau, refused the Israelites passage through their land. Attempting to annex Gilead and attacking other parts of the Promised Land that Lot had rejected, they fought Jephthah in the time of the Judges.

At the start of the Israelite monarchy, Nahash, the Ammonite king, was "determined to reestablish Ammonite dominion over Israelite settlements in Transjordan. He launched an aggressive military campaign around 1020 BC that took him as far north as Jabesh-gilead"—and was turned back by Saul, Israel's eventual first king. When David received the throne, Nahash, whether out of expediency or because he was drawn to the Lord's anointed, became his friend. Yet the tenuous friendship between Israel and Ammon fell apart when Nahash died. His son and successor, Hanun, publicly humiliated a Jewish delegation of sympathy (2 Sam. 10:3–5).

Amos, ministering in the eighth century BC, highlighted the sins of Israel's pagan neighbors, including Ammon, pronouncing divine judgment on them. His Jewish listeners and readers would heartily agree, not knowing they were being led into a divine trap—for they, too, were guilty before a holy God. The Lord said through Amos:

> For three transgressions of the Ammonites,
>   and for four, I will not revoke the punishment,
> because they have ripped open pregnant women in Gilead,
>   that they might enlarge their border.
> So I will kindle a fire in the wall of Rabbah,
>   and it shall devour her strongholds,
> with shouting on the day of battle,
>   with a tempest in the day of the whirlwind;
> and their king shall go into exile,
>   he and his princes together.
>
> Amos 1:13–15

It wasn't just the grisly acts of the Ammonites that spelled their doom; it was their godless attitude toward God's appointed means of the world's redemption: Israel. After the Babylonians sacked Jerusalem in 586 BC, Ammon rejoiced.

This rejection of God's people was not merely uncouth; it was a deliberate rejection of God himself. As God said through Ezekiel:

> Because you have clapped your hands and stamped your feet and rejoiced with all the malice within your soul against the land of Israel, therefore, behold, I have stretched out my hand against you, and will hand you over as plunder to the nations. And I will cut you off from the peoples and will make you perish out of the countries; I will destroy you. Then you will know that I am the LORD.
>
> Ezekiel 25:6–7

And indeed, Ammon was destroyed over time, eventually becoming a pastureland for the nomads of the east.[2] Israel has survived, while nations just as old, such as Ammon, have been relegated to the ash heap of history.

APPLICATION

**Those nations that curse Israel
will be cursed.**

20

Moab

Bitter Fruit

Jeremiah 48:7–8; Ezekiel 25:8–11;
Amos 2:1–3

Moab, like Ben-Ammi, was the son of an incestuous relationship.[1] The children of Moab were prohibited, as were the Ammonites, from entering the assembly of the Lord.[2] Like Edom, they had refused Israel passage to the Promised Land and had hired the false prophet Balaam to curse the people of God, who were God's appointed agents of salvation to the world.

Moab and Israel were perpetual enemies. As Moses said, "But the LORD your God would not listen to Balaam; instead the LORD your God turned the curse into a blessing for you, because the LORD your God loved you. You shall not seek their peace or their prosperity all your days forever" (Deut. 23:5–6). Those who curse Abraham and his seed will be cursed.

Indeed, tiny Moab and Israel were often at one another's throats. The Israelite judge, Ehud, assassinated the repulsive Moabite king, Eglon. Both Saul and David warred against the Moabites. Yet this is not the entire picture. While the nation of Moab consistently opposed God's people, sometimes individuals from Moab made different decisions.

Ruth, for example, chose to join Israel in the unappealing period of the judges, famously declaring to her Israelite mother-in-law, "Your people shall be my people, and your God my God" (Ruth 1:16). God's opposition to the people of Moab had many reasons, but none of them involved race or ethnicity. Anyone, even a Moabite, could follow the Lord. Imperfect as Israel was, it functioned as a beacon calling all of the surrounding nations to righteousness—including tiny Moab.

However, Moabite deities, such as Chemosh, tempted the Israelites to apostasy. Even Solomon built shrines to Chemosh, who sometimes required human sacrifice. But finally, when corporate Moab chose against God's grace, it faced God's judgment. In Jeremiah 48:2, the author declared, "the renown of Moab is no more," adding:

> For, because you trusted in your works and your treasures,
>   you also shall be taken;
> and Chemosh shall go into exile
>   with his priests and his officials.
> The destroyer shall come upon every city,
>   and no city shall escape.
>
> verses 7–8

Amos said God would judge Moab not for anything done to the Jewish people, but for its sins against a neighbor. "I will not revoke the punishment, because [Moab] burned to lime the bones of the king of Edom" (Amos 2:1). This atrocity, committed against a pagan nation, "demonstrates that these judgments are based not on ethnicity but on the universal justice of God."[3] The sentence is fearsome:

> So I will send a fire upon Moab,
>   and it shall devour the strongholds of Kerioth,
> and Moab shall die amid uproar,
>   amid shouting and the sound of the trumpet;
> I will cut off the ruler from its midst,
>   and will kill all its princes with him.
>
> verses 2–3

Ezekiel, speaking as judgment looms, castigates Moab for pretending that the people of God were "like all the other nations" (Ezek. 25:8), thus absolving itself of any responsibility to join, as Ruth did, God's covenant community. Because Moab has rejected God, it will eat the bitter fruit of its rejection (vv. 9–11). The death sentence has been passed.

Nebuchadnezzar, as in so many other cases, is to be the Lord's executioner. And, right on schedule, the Babylonian armies roll in and destroy Moab's proud kingdom, which is never to rise again.

APPLICATION

**Rejecting God's grace brings on
God's judgment.**

21

Egypt

An End beyond the End

Isaiah 19:25; 20:3–6; Jeremiah 46:25–26;
Ezekiel 31:10–11; Revelation 7:9

Evidence of human civilization has been found in Egypt starting in 5000 BC. By the time of the Exodus, Egypt was experiencing a golden age. The New Kingdom "was destined to become probably the most brilliant age in all Egyptian history. . . . An empire soon was to be built which reached from the Fourth Cataract of the Nile to beyond the Euphrates."[1]

Just as the Egyptian empire rose to its zenith over the course of centuries, so its sun set slowly. By the beginning of the seventh century BC, the Assyrians had asserted control over much of Palestine, defeating an Egyptian army in Philistine territory.

Isaiah had a prophecy for Egypt, which worshiped Amon, supposedly the king of the gods. When the Assyrians captured the northern coastal city of Ashdod, the Lord told Isaiah to walk around naked for three years. Then he told Isaiah to prophesy:

> As my servant Isaiah has walked naked and barefoot for three years as a sign and a portent against Egypt and Cush, so shall the king of Assyria lead away the Egyptian captives and the Cushite exiles. . . . And the inhabitants of this coastland will say in that day, "Behold,

this is what has happened to those in whom we hoped and to whom
we fled for help to be delivered from the king of Assyria! And we, how
shall we escape?"

Isaiah 20:3–4, 6

The warning to God's people was clear: do not look to Egypt and its
god Amon for salvation. And indeed, Judah escaped Assyrian control
through *God's* intervention (see Isaiah 36–37).

When Assyria, however, had to contend with the rising Babylonians and
Medes, Pharaoh Neco II moved his army across Palestine again, killing
good King Josiah in the process, and placed the vassal king Jehoiakim
on the throne in Jerusalem.[2]

Yet the prophets of Judah foresaw Egypt's end—as well as the end
beyond the end. Once again, the Lord used Babylon to execute judgment. "Because [Egypt] towered high and set its top among the clouds,
and its heart was proud of its height, I will give it into the hand of
a mighty one of the nations" (Ezek. 31:10–11). Jeremiah added this
prophecy: "Behold, I am bringing punishment upon Amon of Thebes,
and Pharaoh and Egypt and her gods and her kings, upon Pharaoh and
those who trust in him. I will deliver them into the hand of those who
seek their life, into the hand of Nebuchadnezzar king of Babylon and
his officers" (Jer. 46:25–26).

History records that Nebuchadnezzar "met Necho at Carchemish in
605 BC and routed his army completely." Later, Egypt came under the
rule of Persia, then Greece, then Rome, then the house of Islam.[3]

While the Egyptian empire is gone, God's concern for the Egyptian
people has continued. The prophets made the radical point that God
wants the followers of Amon to be the followers of the Lord. Isaiah's
vision encompasses Egypt and more: "In that day Israel will be the third
with Egypt and Assyria, a blessing in the midst of the earth, whom the
Lord of hosts has blessed, saying, 'Blessed be Egypt my people, and
Assyria the work of my hands, and Israel my inheritance'" (Isa. 19:25).
Certainly Egypt has had a significant presence of God's people—both
Jews and Christians—in the intervening centuries.

In the New Testament John the apostle's vision was even broader,
reaching Egypt and beyond: "After this I looked, and behold, a great
multitude that no one could number, from every nation, from all tribes
and peoples and languages, standing before the throne and before the

Lamb, clothed in white robes, with palm branches in their hands" (Rev. 7:9). Truly the blessing of Abraham will one day reach all the nations.

APPLICATION

Are you working to spread the gospel among all the nations of the earth?

22

Nebuchadnezzar's Dream of Earthly Empires

Daniel 2

Nebuchadnezzar, as ruler of the known world, is seemingly secure. He has crushed the Assyrians, sacked Jerusalem, and now directs an empire that outshines all that have gone before it. Yet this incomparable ruler, used by God to carry out judgment on the surrounding nations, is troubled by—of all things—a dream. As Shakespeare said, "Uneasy lies the head that wears a crown."[1]

So Nebuchadnezzar calls on his specially trained wise men to interpret the dream. But Nebuchadnezzar is also a practical man—a man of results. While the ancient world had no trouble believing in the supernatural, Nebuchadnezzar is unwilling to operate by blind faith. He wants evidence. Not only must these wise men tell the king what his disquieting vision means, they must reveal the contents of the dream itself. If they truly have a hotline to the gods, they will be richly rewarded. But if they fail the test, then they will die for deceiving the king. Call it a high-stakes scientific experiment.

The wise men, called Chaldeans, are flabbergasted. "There is not a man on earth who can meet the king's demand, for no great and powerful king has asked such a thing of any magician or enchanter or Chaldean," they complain (see Dan. 2:10).

Furious, Nebuchadnezzar pronounces a death sentence on all the wise men (v. 12), which includes Daniel and his companions. However, Daniel, like Joseph before him, says that God, and God alone, will reveal the answer to the king: "No wise men, enchanters, magicians, or astrologers can show to the king the mystery that the king has asked, but there is a God in heaven who reveals mysteries, and he has made known to King Nebuchadnezzar what will be in the latter days" (vv. 27–28).

Then Daniel describes the content of the dream: Nebuchadnezzar saw a "great image. . . . mighty and of exceeding brightness," with a head of gold, a chest and arms of silver, its middle and thighs of bronze, its legs of iron, and its feet a mix of iron and clay. Then the king saw a stone smash into the statue, collapsing the great image, which crumbled into chaff, blown away by the wind. In its place the stone "became a great mountain and filled the whole earth" (see vv. 31–35).

Then comes the interpretation: Nebuchadnezzar is the head of gold. Three more empires will rise, inferior to Babylon—of silver, bronze, and iron mixed with clay. Bible scholars have identified the silver kingdom as Persia, the bronze as Greece, and the iron and clay as Rome.[2]

Finally, Daniel says, "the God of heaven will set up a kingdom that shall never be destroyed. . . . It shall break in pieces all these kingdoms and bring them to an end, and it shall stand forever" (v. 44).

Christians know this imperishable, triumphant kingdom to be the kingdom of God, as announced by Jesus Christ in the time of Roman domination: "The kingdom of heaven is like a grain of mustard seed that a man took and sowed in his field. It is the smallest of all seeds, but when it has grown it is larger than all the garden plants and becomes a tree, so that the birds of the air come and make nests in its branches" (Matt. 13:31–32).

Babylon rose and fell. Persia rose and fell. Greece rose and fell. Rome rose and fell. The kingdom of God has overturned and outlasted them all.

APPLICATION

**We can rest easy because God
controls world history.**

23

Nebuchadnezzar
A Beastly Judgment

Daniel 4

Nebuchadnezzar, told he is the "head of gold,"[1] is riding high. The emperor *nonpareil* is "at ease in my house and prospering in my palace" (Dan. 4:4). Then he has a frightening dream. In it Nebuchadnezzar sees a gigantic tree in the midst of the earth, its crown reaching heaven. The tree, universally visible, provides shade for the beasts, branches for the birds, and food for all creatures. But then the dream turns dark. A "watcher" comes down from heaven and proclaims, "Chop down the tree and lop off its branches, strip off its leaves and scatter its fruit. Let the beasts flee from under it and the birds from its branches" (v. 14).

Then the dream becomes even more disturbing. The watcher continues, "But leave the stump of its roots in the earth, bound with a band of iron and bronze, amid the tender grass of the field. Let him be wet with the dew of heaven. Let his portion be with the beasts in the grass of the earth. Let his mind be changed from a man's, and let a beast's mind be given to him; and let seven periods of time pass over him" (vv. 15–16).

The dream even comes with its own explanation. The watcher says, "The sentence is by the decree of the watchers, . . . to the end that the living may know that the Most High rules the kingdom of men and gives it to whom he will and sets over it the lowliest of men" (v. 17).

No brutish thug, Nebuchadnezzar is surely one of the brightest men of his age, having "consolidated the power of Babylon from the Persian

Gulf to the Mediterranean, and from the Amanus Mountains to the Sinai."² Yet initially he plays dumb and calls in his wise men again. However, the sorcerers are unable, or perhaps unwilling, to give him the bad news—rightly respecting his explosive temper.

So Nebuchadnezzar asks for the trustworthy Daniel, whom he calls "chief of the magicians." Daniel, probably like the rest, is dismayed by the ominous vision. When pressed, he tells the king what he *doesn't* want to hear: "It is you, O king, who have grown and become strong," Daniel says (v. 22).

> It is a decree of the Most High, . . . that you shall be driven from among men, and your dwelling shall be with the beasts of the field. You shall be made to eat grass like an ox, and you shall be wet with the dew of heaven, and seven periods of time shall pass over you, till you know that the Most High rules the kingdom of men and gives it to whom he will.
>
> verses 24–25

Perhaps remembering the Lord's mercy on Nineveh, Daniel's advice is simple: *Repent.*

A year later, Nebuchadnezzar is on the roof of his palace, overcome with pride. "Is not this great Babylon," he asks no one in particular, "which I have built by my mighty power as a royal residence and for the glory of my majesty?" (v. 30). God hears his boast, and the predicted judgment arrives. Commentators identify Nebuchadnezzar's resulting condition, which lasts seven years, as *boanthropy*,³ a rare psychological disorder in which people believe they are cows. Could anything be more humiliating?

Chastened, eventually Nebuchadnezzar learns his lesson, receiving his considerable faculties back once again. He proclaims: "I, Nebuchadnezzar, praise and extol and honor the King of heaven, for all his works are right and his ways are just; and those who walk in pride he is able to humble" (v. 37).

APPLICATION

**In love, the Lord humbles the
proud in heart.**

24

Babylon

The Writing on the Wall

Isaiah 13:17–22; Daniel 5

Though a repentant Nebuchadnezzar received his personal reprieve,[1] Babylon's days as a world power are numbered. Thus said the prophets, who foresaw God's judgment on the "evil empire" of the sixth century BC. Isaiah prophesied:

> Behold, I am stirring up the Medes against them. . . .
> Their bows will slaughter the young men;
>> they will have no mercy on the fruit of the womb;
>> their eyes will not pity children.
> And Babylon, the glory of kingdoms,
>> the splendor and pomp of the Chaldeans,
> will be like Sodom and Gomorrah
>> when God overthrew them.
> It will never be inhabited
>> or lived in for all generations.
>
> Isaiah 13:17–20

Closer to Babylon's end, Jeremiah proclaims, "For out of the north a nation has come up against her, which shall make her land a desolation, and none shall dwell in it; both man and beast shall flee away" (Jer. 50:3). God tells Habakkuk that after the more wicked Chaldeans judge Judah, they will face their own judgment. If revenge is a dish best served cold, Habakkuk's response is definitely chilly: "I will wait patiently for the day of calamity to come on the nation invading us" (Hab. 3:16 NIV).

Contemporaries might have concluded that the prophets would be waiting a very long time. The city displayed the awe-inspiring Ishtar Gate, "a double gate leading through the double wall of fortifications and adorned with rows of bulls and dragons in enameled, colored brick."[2] According to the Greek historian Herodotus, Nebuchadnezzar had rebuilt an eight-stage ziggurat in the rebuilt temple area of Marduk. Not to be forgotten were the famous Hanging Gardens, one of the seven wonders of the ancient world.[3]

Yet the Lord's timing was perfect. Noting Babylon's destruction of Jerusalem, historian Jack Finegan writes, "The New Babylonian empire . . . was destined to fall, and the decline came rapidly." After Nebuchadnezzar, his son and grandson ruled in brief succession, followed by others, who were not in the royal line. Finally, one Nabonidus was king, from 556–539 BC. His son Belshazzar ruled when Nabonidus was away. Daniel the prophet was on the scene when Babylon's, and Belshazzar's, time was up.[4]

During a royal banquet, Belshazzar and a thousand of his closest friends are drinking wine from the golden vessels of God's temple, praising "the gods of gold and silver, bronze, iron, wood, and stone" (Dan. 5:4). Suddenly what look like the fingers of a human hand appear and write a mysterious message on the plaster wall. As before, none of the wise men can decipher it, so Daniel is called in. "This is the interpretation of the matter," Daniel says: "MENE, God has numbered the days of your kingdom and brought it to an end; TEKEL, you have been weighed in the balances and found wanting; PERES, your kingdom is divided and given to the Medes and Persians" (vv. 26–28).

Babylon falls to the Medes and Persians that very night (vv. 30–31). And in the two and a half millennia since, it has remained desolate, a haunt for jackals and other creatures of the desert.[5]

APPLICATION

No one is above God's justice.

25

The Nations
to Be Blessed

Habakkuk 2:14; Ephesians 2:11–13;
Revelation 19:6–8

Israel, though uniquely called by God, does not represent the terminus of his concern. As God said to Jonah about Nineveh, "Should I not be concerned?" (Jon. 4:11 NIV). Israel was blessed, not simply to enjoy its blessings, but to *be* a blessing. More than that, it serves as a spiritual Rorschach test, applying not just to nations but to individuals. Those peoples and individuals who, like Ruth of Moab, bless the people of God prove that they are open to the blessings of the Lord. Those that curse Israel, however, show themselves to be ripe for judgment.

Nations are judged, forgiven, destroyed, or spared based not only on what they do with Israel but on how they respond to the light they have. Nowhere does the Bible say that this process has ended.

And while the afterlife is definitely a minor theme in the Old Testament, national judgments provide a clear window into eternal issues. As Jesus said, "The men of Nineveh will rise up at the judgment with this generation and condemn it, for they repented at the preaching of Jonah, and behold, something greater than Jonah is here" (Luke 11:32).

God's ultimate desire for Israel and the nations, however, is not judgment, but that they (according to the Westminster Shorter Catechism[1]) might love him, the source of all blessings, and enjoy him forever. On their best days, the prophets understood this. Habakkuk, who longed for God's righteous judgment on the wicked Babylonians, nonetheless prophesied, "For the earth will be filled with the knowledge of the glory of the LORD as the waters cover the sea" (Hab. 2:14).

One day God's purpose will be fulfilled. In the days of Noah,[2] waters covered the earth in judgment. In the future, water signifies the fulfillment of the Lord's prophecy to bless the nations. As the apostle John prophesied:

> Then I heard what sounded like a great multitude, like the roar of rushing waters and like loud peals of thunder, shouting:
>
> "Hallelujah!
>   For our Lord God Almighty reigns.
> Let us rejoice and be glad
>   and give him glory!
> For the wedding of the Lamb has come,
>   and his bride has made herself ready.
> Fine linen, bright and clean,
>   was given her to wear."
>
> Revelation 19:6–8 NIV

Of course biblical scholars say we live amid the tension of the *already* and the *not yet*. The finish line of Habakkuk's prophecy is *not yet*, but we are *already* seeing signs pointing to it. A key marker occurred when Jews from across the Roman Empire heard the Good News as the Spirit was poured out (Acts 2).

The blessing expanded when the Gentiles were included in God's kingdom, as Paul told a group of former worshipers of the goddess Artemis:

> Therefore remember that . . . you Gentiles . . . were at that time separated from Christ, alienated from the commonwealth of Israel and strangers to the covenants of promise, having no hope and without God in the world. But now in Christ Jesus you who once were far off have been brought near by the blood of Christ.
>
> Ephesians 2:11–13

We continue to see signs of God's expanding global blessing in answer to the ancient prophecies. "Though sometimes small in number," reports the authoritative *Operation World* prayer guide, "there are now Christians living and fellowshipping in every country on earth."[3]

APPLICATION

**God's determination to bless the nations
will not be stopped, so those who join him
in this task are automatic winners.**

The Once and Future Kings

26

A Great King

Genesis 49:10; Psalm 2:10–12

When Israel was constituted as a people, the nation had no earthly king to protect it in a very dangerous neighborhood. Abraham was a nomad; Isaac dug wells; Jacob raised sheep. Moses, who led God's people out of Egyptian bondage, was a lawgiver. When settling into the land of promise, Israel was delivered by a series of judges, each specially called by God. Other nations had kings, emperors, and pharaohs, but not tiny Israel. That's because this unique nation, blessed to be a blessing, had only one King—God himself.

Yet the Jewish people looked around at their neighbors and were not content with this arrangement, which seemed highly unstable and required too much day-to-day faith. *They* wanted a king too. The prophet Samuel, the last of the judges, was not pleased, but God told him, "Obey the voice of the people in all that they say to you, for they have not rejected you, but they have rejected me from being king over them" (1 Sam. 8:7).

And so the monarchy began under less than ideal circumstances, but God was not taken by surprise. In fact he had planned for it all along. Jacob, before he passed from the scene, had prophesied hundreds of years before: "The scepter shall not depart from Judah, nor the ruler's staff from between his feet, until tribute comes to him; and to him shall be the obedience of the peoples" (Gen. 49:10).

While the northern kingly lines were eventually obliterated by the Assyrians, Judah's royal line continued right up to the time of Christ. Jacob's prophecy also points to the fact that eventually God's kingdom will encompass much more than the Jewish nation. Of course, in a sense, God already reigns over the nations. He is not a mere Jewish tribal deity. He is Lord over all the earth, worthy of everyone's worship. As the psalmist said,

> God reigns over the nations;
> God sits on his holy throne.
> The princes of the peoples gather
> as the people of the God of Abraham.
> For the shields of the earth belong to God;
> he is highly exalted!
>
> Psalm 47:8–9

But in another sense, God's kingly rule must be acknowledged and received, not only by the Jews but by the far more numerous and mighty Gentiles. It is a kingdom that brings together heaven and earth.

To this end, Israel's earthly sovereign is anointed to be the ideal leader, the focus on earth of the divine plan. In a sense, the king is God's "son" (see 2 Sam. 7:14). Well, Israel's long history displays both good and bad kings, but no perfect ones. Scripture, however, looks forward to an ultimate Son and King, perfect in holiness and power, whom Psalm 2 warns the unbelieving nations to embrace:

> Now therefore, O kings, be wise;
> be warned, O rulers of the earth.
> Serve the LORD with fear,
> and rejoice with trembling.
> Kiss the Son,
> lest he be angry, and you perish in the way,
> for his wrath is quickly kindled.
> Blessed are all who take refuge in him.
>
> verses 10–12

Who is this royal Son of God? The apostles thought they knew the answer.[1]

APPLICATION

**Have you taken refuge
in the divine King?**

27

An Unending Royal Line

2 Samuel 7:1–16; Psalm 89:26–27;
Matthew 1; Revelation 11:15

In the irreverent movie spoof *History of the World: Part 1*, a debauched
Mel Brooks says with an impish gleam in his eye, "It's good to be the
king." But while ruling as monarch may be "good" in terms of short-term
power or pleasure, it is not necessarily good for one's longevity.

This was certainly the case in the Northern Kingdom of Israel. In
the roughly two centuries of its existence, Israel had nineteen kings,
spread over nine family dynasties. The first dynasty, of Jeroboam, lasted
twenty-two years, ended by assassination. The next dynasty, of Baasha,
lasted twenty-four years, also ending by assassination. Then followed
dynasties that lasted seven days, forty-four years, eighty-nine years, one
month, twelve years, twenty years, and ten years, respectively. All ended
via assassination or military defeat.[1]

While the Southern Kingdom had twenty monarchs of its own,[2] it had
but *one* dynasty—that of David, the shepherd boy who slew a giant and
established the standard for all Jewish kings. This was because David—
unlike the others—refused to put himself first. Instead, he put God first.

From the time of Moses, the Lord had dwelt with his people in a special
way via the ark of the covenant, which was housed in the tabernacle, a
portable place of worship. After David had captured much of the land
God had promised to the Hebrew people, Israel was finally ready to
defeat the pagan counterfeits and reach the nations for the one true God.

David had built himself a royal residence but was struck by the incongruity that God had no permanent abode on earth: "See now, I dwell in a house of cedar, but the ark of God dwells in a tent" (2 Sam. 7:2).

The Lord was pleased with David's desire to build the temple, telling his humble king:

> I took you from the pasture, from following the sheep, that you should be prince over my people Israel. . . . And I will make for you a great name. . . . And I will appoint a place for my people Israel and will plant them, so that they may dwell in their own place and be disturbed no more. . . . Moreover, the LORD declares to you that the LORD will make you a house. . . . Your throne shall be established forever.
>
> 2 Samuel 7:8–11, 16

David's dynasty will last forever, the Lord promises. God will always have his "son" on the throne (see Ps. 89:26–27).

These unilateral promises of God to David constitute one of several divinely instituted covenants in the Bible—the Davidic covenant. A covenant is "a relationship that commits people to one another, God to God's people, and people to God."[3] The Davidic covenant is repeated several places in the Scriptures, such as in Psalm 132, as if God's people are reminding him of the terms of the contract he wrote up and asking him to keep his word.

Fidelity is not a problem for God, though he keeps his word in a way that most do not foresee. Judah falls to the Babylonians, but the line continues (see Matthew 1). Eventually One who answers to the titles Son of David (see Luke 18:38, 41) and Son of God (see Matt. 16:16; John 1:45–49) appears. Of him the heavenly choir sings, "The kingdom of the world has become the kingdom of our Lord and of his Christ, and he shall reign forever and ever" (Rev. 11:15).

APPLICATION

Ultimately only one kingdom matters.

28

A Shoot from the Stump of Jesse

Isaiah 11:1–10

When society appears to be on the verge of collapse and the wolves are at the door, people naturally look to their leaders for deliverance. If those leaders appear to be overmatched by the challenges of the day, citizens pine for earlier ones who brought their nation through times of great peril. In the United States, liberals look to FDR; conservatives, to Reagan.

Ancient Israel longed for David—and not without reason. King David had inaugurated a brief golden age in Israel, defeating the Philistines, Moab, Ammon, and Syria, extending the tiny nation's territory all the way to the Euphrates. His greatness was summed up in the simple statement: "And the LORD gave victory to David wherever he went" (2 Sam. 8:14).

Of course a realist would argue that David rose to power when the grip of global empires such as Assyria and Egypt was loosening. Later, when in the providence of God the superpowers came roaring back into the Promised Land, the divided kingdoms of Israel and Judah faced calamity and eventual destruction. In these times of national insecurity, the Jewish people naturally looked to a savior—to David.

With the Assyrians at the gates of Jerusalem, Isaiah understood this longing. The region would be mowed down, but an heir of David the son of Jesse would do what no mere human ruler ever could—inaugurate a Spirit-powered reign of righteousness and peace.

> There shall come forth a shoot from the stump of Jesse,
> and a branch from his roots shall bear fruit.

> And the Spirit of the LORD shall rest upon him,
>> the Spirit of wisdom and understanding,
>> the Spirit of counsel and might,
>> the Spirit of knowledge and the fear of the LORD. . . .
>
> The wolf shall dwell with the lamb,
>> and the leopard shall lie down with the young goat,
> and the calf and the lion and the fattened calf together;
>> and a little child shall lead them.
> The cow and the bear shall graze;
>> their young shall lie down together;
>> and the lion shall eat straw like the ox.
> The nursing child shall play over the hole of the cobra,
>> and the weaned child shall put his hand on the adder's den.
> They shall not hurt or destroy
>> in all my holy mountain;
> for the earth shall be full of the knowledge of the LORD
>> as the waters cover the sea.

In that day the root of Jesse, who shall stand as a signal for the peoples—of him shall the nations inquire, and his resting place shall be glorious.

Isaiah 11:1–2, 6–10

What the people need, Isaiah prophesies, is not merely protection from Assyria or Babylon. Even David could not provide that. What they need is a greater David who will provide true security and rest. And God, who ever supplies the needs of his people, has already begun to fulfill this prophecy, in the ultimate Son of David, Jesus Christ. "And when Jesus was baptized, immediately he went up from the water, and behold, the heavens were opened to him, and he saw the Spirit of God descending like a dove and coming to rest on him; and behold, a voice from heaven said, 'This is my beloved Son, with whom I am well pleased'" (Matt. 3:16–17).

APPLICATION

**Only the Son of God can provide the
security we need.**

29

A Future David

Jeremiah 33:14–16, 20–22

Jeremiah, known as "the weeping prophet," is eyewitness to the nation's fast approaching disaster. Worse still is that, as with the mythical Cassandra, his warnings will go unheeded. In fact he faces derision, persecution, and eventual death. Yet God promises to be with him through it all: "They will fight against you, but they shall not prevail against you, for I am with you, declares the LORD, to deliver you" (Jer. 1:19).

Seemingly the fall of Jerusalem and the smashing of the temple by the fist of Nebuchadnezzar and the Babylonians mark the end for God's people. God's promise to David of an unending royal line appears to be a pointless mistake—or some kind of cosmic joke. Yet Jeremiah, tortured in body and in soul, somehow sees a coming restoration that shatters the boundaries of human expectation. A descendent of David, who briefly united Israel and Judah under his kingly rule, will one day restore the worship of the one true God. Like Isaiah before him, Jeremiah (speaking for God) calls this man a "Branch": "I will cause a righteous Branch to spring up for David, and he shall execute justice and righteousness in the land. In those days Judah will be saved, and Jerusalem will dwell securely. And this is the name by which it will be called: 'The LORD is our righteousness'" (33:15–16).

The term *branch* means "that which 'shoots up,' or 'sprouts' from the root of a tree, or from a decayed tree."[1] The Davidic line may wither or seemingly die, but a root *will* spring up. That branch will have the exalted name, "The Lord is our righteousness," and he will save the people.

This prophecy must seem too good to be true to a people who are headed for exile, so God through Jeremiah reassures them: "If you can break my covenant with the day and my covenant with the night, so that day and night will not come at their appointed time, then also my covenant with David my servant may be broken, so that he shall not have a son to reign on his throne" (vv. 20–21).

But for six hundred long years, the promise seemed to come to naught. In the time of Christ, the Jewish people are eager to see the Branch. They have in mind a human descendent of David who will rout the Romans and reestablish the kingdom in all its glory. Yet Jesus, referring to Psalm 110, tells them they have set the bar of expectation not too high but too low.

> And as Jesus taught in the temple, he said, "How can the scribes say that the Christ is the son of David? David himself, in the Holy Spirit, declared,
>
> > 'The Lord said to my Lord,
> > Sit at my right hand,
> >   until I put your enemies under your feet.'
>
> David himself calls him Lord. So how is he his son?" And the great throng heard him gladly.
>
> Mark 12:35–37

The Son of David, Jesus says, is no mere man, even a great man, such as David. He is in fact David's Lord. He truly is "the Lord . . . our righteousness," as Jeremiah said. This was the understanding of the early church, which affirmed "Christ Jesus, who became to us . . . righteousness" (1 Cor. 1:30).

APPLICATION

**God's answers are better than
our prayers.**

30

The Son of Man Given Dominion

Daniel 7:13–14; Mark 14:61–64;
Revelation 1:13; 14:14

Many people have their favorite terms for Jesus, the son of Joseph and Mary. Some call him Jesus Christ or Messiah. Others call him Rabbi, Lord, or Savior. Yet Jesus's favorite self-designation was the cryptic Son of Man, as in "Foxes have holes, and birds of the air have nests, but the Son of Man has nowhere to lay his head" (Matt. 8:20) and "Who do people say that the Son of Man is?" (16:13).

In fact the New Testament suggests he used the title about eighty times for himself, though none of his contemporaries called him by it. Ezekiel, unique among the Old Testament authors, applied the term to himself more than ninety times.[1] The term first appears in Numbers 23:19, emphasizing the distance between the Creator and the created: "God is not man, that he should lie, or a son of man, that he should change his mind." Job 25:6 employs it to highlight the lowliness of humanity, saying "man . . . is a maggot, and the son of man . . . is a worm." David, the author of Psalm 8, while agreeing with the distance between man and God, injects a clearer note of human dignity: "What is man that you are mindful of him, and the son of man that you care for him? Yet you have made him a little lower than the heavenly beings and crowned him with glory and honor" (vv. 4–5).

The exiled prophet Daniel combined the term with the coming kingdom of God. After his grand prophecy of various human empires (Dan. 7:1–8),[2] Daniel announces an ultimate kingdom:

> With the clouds of heaven
>   there came one like a son of man,
> and he came to the Ancient of Days
>   and was presented before him.
> And to him was given dominion
>   and glory and a kingdom,
> that all peoples, nations, and languages
>   should serve him;
> his dominion is an everlasting dominion,
>   which shall not pass away,
> and his kingdom one
>   that shall not be destroyed.
>
> verses 13–14

This passage takes the dignity of its subject, "one like a son of man," to a whole new level. This "son of man" stands before God and receives glory and an indestructible, everlasting kingdom and dominion over all nations, to an extent David never realized. Many Jewish commentators have identified this exalted figure as the Messiah.

Yet he is not merely the Messiah, God's new David. Neither is he a little lower than the angels. No, he comes with the clouds of heaven, receiving honors that belong to God alone.

When Jesus is interrogated by a kangaroo court of Jewish leaders, the high priest attempts to entrap him, asking, "Are you the Christ, the Son of the Blessed?" (Mark 14:61). In Jewish eyes, it was one thing to claim to be the Messiah. Such a statement would bring down the wrath of Rome. But to claim to be "the Son of the Blessed" was to invite the wrath of God.

Yet Jesus answered affirmatively to both titles, referring to Daniel's (Jewish) vision for corroboration: "I am, and you will see the Son of Man seated at the right hand of Power, and coming with the clouds of heaven" (v. 62). Jesus was executed by Rome for his claim to be a king; he was done away with by Jews, however, on the charge of blasphemy. The high priest said: "What further witnesses do we need? You have heard his blasphemy. What is your decision" (vv. 63–64)?

What is *your* decision about the new David? Before you decide, remember that Daniel's prophecy awaits ultimate fulfillment, when "one like a son of man" comes to judge the church and the world (see Rev. 1:13; 14:14).

APPLICATION

**The divine Son of Man has come and is coming,
closing the gap between God and man.**

Jesus—
First Advent

31

The Virgin Birth of God

Isaiah 7:14; 9:6; Matthew 1:18–25

Joseph, a carpenter living in a forgotten backwater called Nazareth, is looking forward to spending his life with Mary and raising a family with her. Until the wedding day, she is betrothed to him. The days pass quickly and joyfully as the wedding approaches.

Then one day Mary calls Joseph aside with the most shocking news possible. This beautiful virgin girl says that she is pregnant. Joseph's field of vision momentarily goes black, and his knees buckle. Faintly he hears Mary say that the child is from the Holy Spirit and that she has been faithful to Joseph. He has never known Mary to be a liar and he believes in God's miraculous power as much as anyone—but not *this* story.

Rather than drag Mary's name through the mud, Joseph decides to divorce her quietly. That night, however, he has a dream. An angel of the Lord appears with a message: "Joseph, son of David, do not fear to take Mary as your wife, for that which is conceived in her is from the Holy Spirit. She will bear a son, and you shall call his name Jesus, for he will save his people from their sins" (see Matt. 1:18–25).

When Joseph wakes up, all has changed. Joseph ditches his skepticism and takes Mary as his *virgin* wife and steels himself to defend her honor when the whispers inevitably begin.[1] Certainly it was a convincing dream, but what explains Joseph's complete and sudden about-face?

Matthew, the Gospel writer, says succinctly: "All this took place to fulfill what the Lord had spoken by the prophet: 'Behold, the virgin shall conceive and bear a son, and they shall call his name Immanuel' (which means, God with us)" (vv. 19–20).

Likely Joseph knew this prophecy, which appears in Isaiah 7:14. Critics have said that the word translated "virgin" in Isaiah, *alma*, actually means a young woman of marriageable age, and that the prophecy was fulfilled in the life of Isaiah himself, in the birth of his own son, as a sign that God would quickly defeat Judah's enemies.[2]

Yet this is not the whole story. Jews in Joseph's time probably saw Isaiah 7:14 as both fulfilled in the prophet's life and also as a larger messianic prediction. The Septuagint, a Greek translation of the Old Testament widely circulated in the first century, translates the Hebrew term using the Greek word *parthenos*, which means "virgin."

Therefore Jews such as Joseph viewed the prediction as having a larger, miraculous fulfillment—Immanuel, *God*, would be with them. On reflection, this prophecy may have reinforced the angel's amazing words to Joseph's troubled heart.

It is not surprising that many Jews would combine this prophecy about Immanuel with Isaiah 9:6, which also looks ahead to the birth of a divine Child: "For to us a child is born, . . . and his name shall be called Wonderful Counselor, Mighty God, Everlasting Father, Prince of Peace."

This coming child, Isaiah says, is born of a virgin because he is God himself. No wonder Joseph was so willing to accept Mary's story. The question is, are *we*?

APPLICATION

**Believing God sometimes means
being willing to look foolish.**

32

The Star

Numbers 24:17; Matthew 2:1–11

While some people stumble at the Bible's account of Balaam's donkey being enabled to speak the word of God (Num. 22:22–35), I find the Lord's decision to prophesy through a pagan diviner just as mind-blowing. Employed by the Moabite King Balak to curse Israel before the people of God take possession of the Promised Land, Balaam instead is caused to *bless* them three times (22:1–24:25). During his final oracle, Balaam prophesies:

> I see him, but not now;
> I behold him, but not near:
> a star shall come out of Jacob,
> and a scepter shall rise out of Israel;
> it shall crush the forehead of Moab
> and break down all the sons of Sheth.
>
> Numbers 24:17

In much of the ancient world, of course, stars were thought to foretell or highlight great events, such as the founding of empires or the birth of emperors. Josephus, the first-century Jewish historian, "noted astral phenomena during the fall of Jerusalem in AD 70."[1] The Bible, while condemning astrology, appears to give the celestial bodies a role in communicating God's truth to mankind (see, for example, Gen. 1:14, Ps. 19:1–4; Matt. 24:29–30). Medieval Jews saw Balaam's prophecy of a royal star as pointing to the Messiah.[2]

Likely the early Christians, many of whom were Jews, did as well. Matthew's Gospel, the most Jewish of the four canonical accounts of the life and ministry of Christ, is the only one to note the appearance of a royal star, which scholars note signifies a messianic individual.[3] Yet this passage indicates that non-Jewish Magi from the east, not the Jewish religious or political leaders, first understood the star's significance.

> Now after Jesus was born . . . in the days of Herod the king, behold, wise men from the east came to Jerusalem, saying, "Where is he who has been born king of the Jews? For we saw his star when it rose and have come to worship him." . . . Then Herod summoned the wise men secretly and ascertained from them what time the star had appeared. . . . After listening to the king, they went on their way. And behold, the star that they had seen when it rose went before them until it came to rest over the place where the child was. When they saw the star, they rejoiced exceedingly with great joy. And going into the house they saw the child with Mary his mother, and they fell down and worshiped him.
>
> Matthew 2:1–2, 7–11

Commentators identify magi (translated as "wise men" in the ESV) in the ancient world as more than pagan magicians: "Some of them were learned men in general, who studied the physical world and were knowledgeable about many things, including the stars. Magi were often court astronomers who were consulted by the rulers of the day for guidance in affairs of state."[4] Daniel fulfilled this role in Babylon, and it may be that these "wise men" came from the ancient land between the Tigris and Euphrates.

Even more mysterious is the star itself. Astronomers such as Johannes Kepler have struggled to identify both its nature and the date of its appearance.[5] There are three main theories about the star:[6] that it was (1) a supernova, (2) a comet, or (3) a rare planetary conjunction. Each might have appeared in a constellation that pointed to a king. While there are pros and cons with each theory, Scripture does not definitively resolve the mystery, probably because the point is not to dissect the star, but, with the Magi, to worship the King whom it signifies.

APPLICATION

**Do you worship the royal star
or the royal Jesus?**

33

Born in Bethlehem

Micah 5:1–2; Matthew 2:4–5; Luke 2:11

During the prophetic ministry of Micah, around 700 BC, tiny Judah was being threatened by the snarling and resurgent Assyrian empire. Israel, the Northern Kingdom, was already on Assyria's chopping block. Was Judah next for King Sennacherib? The nation's prospects, humanly speaking, were bleak.

Into this darkness, Micah shined a prophetic word both of judgment and of hope. The people had sinned but they would be delivered. And only God would get the credit. Isaiah 36 and 37 tell the amazing story of how the Lord smote the blasphemous Assyrian army, delivering Jerusalem, the city founded by David, without human help. Yet Micah looks far beyond temporal victories to eternal realities.

> Now muster your troops, O daughter of troops;
>   siege is laid against us;
> with a rod they strike the judge of Israel
>   on the cheek.
> But you, O Bethlehem Ephrathah,
>   who are too little to be among the clans of Judah,
> from you shall come forth for me
>   one who is to be ruler in Israel,
> whose coming forth is from of old,
>   from ancient days.
>
> Micah 5:1–2

Amid the very real military threats of the day, Micah turns his attention to Bethlehem, a small but strategic city outside Jerusalem. It sat atop a mountain 2,654 feet high,[1] where Rachel was buried, Ruth lived, and David was born and anointed as king. The name might mean "house of Lahama," a Canaanite goddess, or "house of bread." Micah is careful to distinguish this Bethlehem from another one, near Nazareth (Ephrathah is the name of its Judean district).[2]

He notes that Bethlehem, like Judah in the wider world, is insignificant. It is too small even to be considered a clan. A clan in ancient Israel included at least three generations and was "comprised of extended families which shared a common and recognizable lineage"[3]—yet Bethlehem is too inconsequential even for this modest designation. It has long been the scene not of great world events, but of shepherds tending their sheep, as in David's early career, the lowly workers who were "keeping watch over their flock by night" when Jesus was born (Luke 2:8), and even today.

Yet size and strength matter little in God's economy. Tiny Bethlehem is to be the birthplace of a greater David, "one who is to be ruler in Israel," whom first-century Jews knew to be the coming Messiah. A false king, Herod, "inquired of [the religious experts] where the Christ was to be born. They told him, 'In Bethlehem of Judea, for so it is written by the prophet'" (Matt. 2:4–5).

It was a conviction these experts would hold for decades. Later, when the people were beginning to follow a certain Jew from the Galilean city of Nazareth, other Jewish leaders—apparently unaware that Jesus was actually born in Bethlehem—dismissed him because he supposedly did not fit Micah's prophecy. "Are you from Galilee too?" they sarcastically asked a sympathetic Nicodemus. "Search and see that no prophet arises from Galilee" (John 7:52).

Contrary to human expectation but in accord with the ancient prophecy, an angel announces to Bethlehem's shepherds, "For unto you is born this day in the city of David a Savior, who is Christ the Lord" (Luke 2:11). Deliverance, now as then, depends on *God's* strength not our own.

APPLICATION

Seeking God's glory sometimes makes no sense from a human perspective.

34

Simeon and Anna

Luke 2:22–38

Forty days after Jesus's birth, Joseph and Mary have long since left Bethlehem's manger and are trekking to Jerusalem to dedicate their firstborn son to the Lord, as the Law requires (Lev. 12:3–4). The angels' messages to Zechariah, Mary, Joseph, and the shepherds are warm memories but already beginning to fade a bit. Mary and Joseph are learning the routines of parenthood without the benefit of a honeymoon or even a proper wedding.

The Magi, unlooked for, have not yet arrived, the natal star not yet visible or noticed.[1] Money is tight. After such an auspicious beginning, life for the family of Joseph is quickly acquiring a deflating kind of normality. This should be no surprise, as the people are under a grinding and seemingly hopeless Roman domination.

But suddenly the gathering clouds part while Mary and Joseph are in the temple. An old man, Simeon—named after one of Jacob's twelve sons—approaches the chosen couple, a look of joy, relief, and authority etched on his ancient face. Simeon, whose name means "hear," has indeed been listening, "waiting for the consolation of Israel." The Spirit has already told "righteous and devout" Simeon that he will not die until he has seen the Savior. Throwing caution and convention to the winds, Simeon picks up the baby as if he knows him—and indeed he does (see Luke 2:25–28).

> Lord, now you are letting your servant depart in peace,
>   according to your word;
> for my eyes have seen your salvation
>   that you have prepared in the presence of all peoples,

> a light for revelation to the Gentiles,
> and for glory to your people Israel.
>
> verses 29–32

Through untold long years, Simeon has been waiting for the Messiah: expectantly, quietly, perhaps painfully. And finally, the Anointed One has come. Simeon needs nothing now—not even life itself. The dawn of salvation for the world is enough.

Then Simeon blesses the couple, who marvel at his encouraging words. Yet Simeon sounds a discordant note: Not everyone will rejoice. Perhaps reflecting on his own long wait, the old man warns Mary cryptically, "a sword will pierce through your own soul also" (v. 35).

Before Joseph and Mary can process these unsettling words, however, Anna, who has been a widow longer than most people have been alive, steps forward. Anna, whose name means "grace" or "favor," has seen little according to worldly standards. She has lived at the temple for decades, perhaps out of necessity. Yet the long years in Jerusalem, separated from the comforts of family life, have not made old Anna bitter; to the contrary, she prays and fasts as easily as others breathe. And hers is no grim legalism. This well-known Jerusalem saint has also been waiting patiently for God to fulfill his promise, and she shares her joy with a couple that desperately needs to hear it (see vv. 36–38).

Two millennia later we know little about Simeon and Anna. Anna's words, for that matter, are not even recorded for us. Why, then, do these two old saints pop up like prairie dogs, only to quickly disappear from our view?

Though they add little to our knowledge of Jesus, they provide windows into the character of faith, which can often be lonely. Their rejoicing and encouragement come only after years of private waiting. And though history-changing events have begun to unfold, Anna and Simeon teach us that God cares not only about the world but also about each one of us.

APPLICATION

**How patiently do you await the fulfillment
of God's promises?**

35

Kings Will Bring Him Gifts

Psalm 72:5–11; Isaiah 60:5, 11; 66:12;
Matthew 2:1–11

One of the great hymns of Christendom is "Jesus Shall Reign Where'er the Sun," written in 1719 by Isaac Watts. Though it contains dashes of British cultural imperialism that no longer pass liturgical muster today, it has been ranked the tenth most popular hymn ever composed.[1] This masterpiece continues to inspire the faithful:

> Jesus shall reign where'er the sun
> Does his successive journeys run;
> His kingdom stretch from shore to shore,
> Till moons shall wax and wane no more.
>
> Behold the islands with their kings,
> And Europe her best tribute brings;
> From north to south the princes meet,
> To pay their homage at His feet.
>
> People and realms of every tongue
> Dwell on His love with sweetest song;
> And infant voices shall proclaim
> Their early blessings on His Name.[2]

Watts was an innovator, writing hymns that did not simply repeat the biblical psalms verbatim. But they did, like "Jesus Shall Reign," borrow freely, giving them their peculiar power.

In *Notes on the Methodist Hymn Book*, G. J. Stevenson describes an occasion in 1862 in the South Sea Islands when King George of Great Britain met with local leaders, who were coming under British law:

> Around him were seated old chiefs and warriors who had shared with him the dangers and fortunes of many a battle—men whose eyes were dim, and whose powerful frames were bowed down with the weight of years. But old and young alike rejoiced together in the joys of that day, their faces most of them radiant with Christian joy, love, and hope. It would be impossible to describe the deep feeling manifested when the solemn service began, by the entire audience singing Dr. Watts' hymn.[3]

The hymn was born in the prophecy of Psalm 72, which points to Solomon and a King beyond David's royal son.

> May they fear you while the sun endures,
>   and as long as the moon, throughout all generations!
> May he be like rain that falls on the mown grass,
>   like showers that water the earth!
> In his days may the righteous flourish,
>   and peace abound, till the moon be no more! . . .
> May the kings of Tarshish and of the coastlands
>   render him tribute;
> may the kings of Sheba and Seba
>   bring gifts!
> May all kings fall down before him,
>   all nations serve him!
>
> Psalm 72:5–7, 10–11

The prophet Isaiah also foresaw a coming Jewish King who would receive "the wealth of nations" (see Isa. 60:5, 11; 66:12). Of course, after the destruction of Jerusalem in 586 BC, such predictions seemed to be mere examples of Jewish hubris—or dementia.

Then, according to Matthew 2:1–11, some Magi arrive from the east, seeking the One "who has been born king of the Jews" (v. 2). In a partial down payment on the ancient prophecy, they come to the house laden with gifts: "Then, opening their treasures, they offered him gifts, gold and frankincense and myrrh" (v. 11). Some have speculated that these three gifts correspond to the "three kings" who gave them, but we don't really know. We do know that these representatives of the nations that have been blessed by Abraham's seed are only doing what is right. They return the favor. Until the King returns and the moon waxes and wanes no more, we are to do the same.

APPLICATION

What gift do you offer to the One who has been born king of the Jews?

36

Slaughter of the Innocents

Exodus 1:15–16, 22; Jeremiah 31:15;
Matthew 2:16–18

Matthew, the former Jewish tax collector for Rome, penned the most Jewish of the four Gospels, showing over and over how Jesus, fulfilling prophecy, is Israel's rightful Messiah and King. Matthew 1:18–2:23 is his account of Jesus's infancy. It is constructed around five Old Testament texts: (1) 1:18–25 reflects Isaiah 7:14, his miraculous birth; (2) 2:6 reflects 1 Samuel 16:4, his birthplace; (3) 2:13–15 reflects Hosea 11:1, his call as God's son; (4) 2:16–18 reflects Exodus 1:15–16, 22, and Jeremiah 31:15, the slaughter of the innocents; and (5) 2:19–23 reflects Exodus 6:6–8, the promised return from Egypt.[1]

These texts, according to Matthew, prove that Jesus is the fulfillment of both Jewish prophecy and Jewish national experience. We will focus here on the fourth prophecy or type, the slaughter of the innocents.

The Magi from the east, having worshiped the baby Jesus and given him their royal gifts, are warned in a dream not to return to the evil King Herod, who seeks to snuff out the child's life.

Herod, believing the child is still in Bethlehem, is enraged that the Magi have left town without telling him the precise location of the young king. To ensure that he gets the right one, Herod orders his thugs to murder "all the male children in Bethlehem and in all that region who were two years old or under, according to the time that he had ascertained from the wise men" (Matt. 2:16). It is a wantonly brutal act, one of many, tragically, that have occurred throughout human history. However, this one, unlike most of the others, was prophesied hundreds of years before.

First, it echoes the murder of Hebrew males in Egypt during the time of Moses. Just as Moses was rescued via divine intervention to lead his people, so is Jesus. The parallels with Israel's experience don't end there. When Jerusalem was soon to be destroyed by the Babylonians, Jeremiah prophesied:

> Thus says the LORD:
> "A voice is heard in Ramah,
>   lamentation and bitter weeping.
> Rachel is weeping for her children;
>   she refuses to be comforted for her children,
>   because they are no more."
>
> Jeremiah 31:15

The immediate fulfillment came when Jewish sons died or were carried off into exile. Ramah is a town a few miles north of Jerusalem, on the road to Bethlehem, where Rachel was buried. The prediction sounds a discordant note in the middle of Jeremiah's joyous account in chapter 31 of the coming new covenant.[2]

Just as suffering is mixed with joy in the prediction, so it is in the fulfillment. Just as innocent children were slaughtered during the long years of waiting for the Messiah, so they are destroyed when he finally arrives. Herod, standing in for the serpent, is seeking to strike the Son of Eve on the heel.[3] Matthew 2:16–18 is no mere prophecy proof text. It is evidence of a spiritual war that has gone on since time began.

APPLICATION

Often suffering accompanies blessing.

37

Called Out of Egypt

Hosea 11:1; Matthew 2:14–15

After Jesus is born and the wise men have come and gone, an angel warns Joseph in a dream that a jealous Herod is seeking to kill the young King of the Jews.[1] The Gospel writer Matthew reports, "And [Joseph] rose and took the child and his mother by night and departed to Egypt and remained there until the death of Herod. This was to fulfill what the Lord had spoken by the prophet, 'Out of Egypt I called my son'" (Matt. 2:14–15).

The verse Matthew quotes from is Hosea 11:1, which reads in full: "When Israel was a child, I loved him, and out of Egypt I called my son." Most Bible scholars admit that Hosea 11:1 is not a predictive prophecy in the classical sense, and that the prophet probably didn't even know that this poetic verse would one day be considered a fulfilled prophecy. Hosea, who elsewhere *does* announce predictive prophecies,[2] is simply and artistically recounting the Lord's love for Israel, who is his "son." In what sense, then, is this verse *fulfilled*, beginning with the sudden evacuation to Egypt of Jesus and his family, who became refugees in the middle of the night? Why isn't the flight to Egypt simply another random and regrettable event of ancient history?

The Jewish people, unlike the surrounding nations, were *people of history*. They did not believe in endless cycles of birth and rebirth, as the pagans did. They believed in *teleology*, that there is a purpose for the things that happen. They believed history was *going somewhere* and that *they* were somehow bound up in the fate of the world, and that God was actively working *through* their history to redeem mankind. And because God has a dependable and righteous character, he just might work similarly in different historical events.

Many Jews in Jesus's day, for example, would recognize "a correspondence between New and Old Testament events, based on a conviction of the unchanging character of the principles of God's working."[3] The flight to Egypt of Jesus and his family was not predicted, but just as powerfully, it reflects a key event in the life of Israel, for whom Jesus served as a substitute—and sinless—"son" of God. In his divinely planned life, Jesus was recapitulating key episodes in the nation's history.

Certainly key to Jews all over the world, then and now, is the nation's exodus from Egypt. God's people were originally sent to Egypt to escape death through famine, just as Jesus was sent to Egypt to escape death through assassination. The nation was called out of Egypt to serve the Lord and display his glory, just as Jesus was sent back to the Promised Land to bless the world as God had originally intended. G. K. Beale and D. A. Carson note that these were "too striking a set of parallels for Matthew to attribute them to chance. God clearly was at work orchestrating the entire series of events."[4]

Prophecy, as has been said many times, not only *foretells*. It also *forth tells*. Such forth-telling provides believers in an uncertain world with the assurance that God truly is in control.

APPLICATION

How have you seen God providentially orchestrating the details of your life?

Jesus—Life and Ministry

38

Elijah's Return

Isaiah 40:1–3; Malachi 3:1–2; 4:5–6;
Matthew 11:7–15

Isaiah, witness to God's protection of Judah from Assyria around 700 BC, predicts nonetheless the long exile in Babylon as God's judgment for the nation's sin. But he doesn't leave it there. Isaiah also predicts the people's return to the land of promise:

> Comfort, comfort my people, says your God.
> Speak tenderly to Jerusalem,
>   and cry to her
> that her warfare is ended,
>   that her iniquity is pardoned,
> that she has received from the LORD's hand
>   double for all her sins.
> A voice cries:
> "In the wilderness prepare the way of the LORD;
>   make straight in the desert a highway for our God."
>
> Isaiah 40:1–3

And of course the Lord eventually leads the people back through the desert, though they never regain their former national glory. By the time of Malachi, the final prophet, in 400 BC, the people are depressed. The promises of God seem to have failed. But Malachi assures them that God has not forgotten, he is coming, and his messenger will come—echoing Isaiah—to prepare the way.

> Behold, I send my messenger, and he will prepare the way before me. And the Lord whom you seek will suddenly come to his temple; and the messenger of the covenant in whom you delight, behold, he is coming, says the LORD of hosts. But who can endure the day of his coming, and who can stand when he appears? . . . Behold, I will send you Elijah the prophet before the great and awesome day of the LORD comes.
>
> Malachi 3:1–2; 4:5

Then four long centuries pass for the people of God. Persian domination gives way to Greek domination, followed by Roman domination. Where is the messenger, and where is the Lord?

Suddenly a man named John appears, with "a garment of camel's hair and a leather belt around his waist, and his food was locusts and wild honey" (Matt. 3:4). This austere desert lifestyle mirrors that of Elijah the Tishbite (2 Kings 1:8).[1] Like Elijah, John preaches a message of repentance and reform. The people know a prophet is among them, though they aren't quite sure who he is.

> As the people were in expectation, and all were questioning in their hearts concerning John, . . . John answered them all, saying, "I baptize you with water, but he who is mightier than I is coming, the strap of whose sandals I am not worthy to untie. He will baptize you with the Holy Spirit and fire."
>
> Luke 3:15–16

Clearly, though John elsewhere denies being the literal person of Elijah (John 1:21), he fulfills the role of Elijah, "turn[ing] the hearts of fathers to their children and the hearts of children to their fathers" (Mal. 4:6). Jesus has no doubt about John's identity.

> Jesus began to speak to the crowds concerning John: . . . "What then did you go out to see? A prophet? Yes, I tell you, and more than a prophet. This is he of whom it is written,
>
> > 'Behold, I send my messenger before your face,
> > who will prepare your way before you.' . . .

"For all the Prophets and the Law prophesied until John, and if you are willing to accept it, he is Elijah who is to come. He who has ears to hear, let him hear."

Matthew 11:7–10, 13–15

John is the messenger, Jesus says, and *I* am the Lord.

APPLICATION

Conviction of sin accompanies faith in Christ.

39

"The Spirit of the Lord Is upon Me"

Isaiah 42:7; 61:1–2; Matthew 11:5; Luke 4:18–21

After returning from Egyptian exile, Joseph and his family settle in Nazareth, "a very humble village . . . not mentioned in the Hebrew Bible nor by Josephus."[1] After Jesus grows to adulthood and is just beginning his ministry, his fame begins to spread. He goes to the synagogue in Nazareth to make the formal announcement. Standing up, he reads from the scroll:

> The Spirit of the Lord is upon me,
> because he has anointed me
> to proclaim good news to the poor.
> He has sent me to proclaim liberty to the captives
> and recovering of sight to the blind,
> to set at liberty those who are oppressed,
> to proclaim the year of the Lord's favor.
>
> Luke 4:18–19

With all eyes on him, Jesus then provides the shocking interpretation: "Today this Scripture has been fulfilled in your hearing" (v. 21). Jesus was reading from Isaiah 61:1–2, when the prophet looked beyond the coming Babylonian exile to the people's miraculous return to the land. In a sense, the prophecy was already fulfilled, as Jesus knew full well, so why did he claim to be the ultimate fulfillment, hundreds of years later?

On the surface, Isaiah 61:1–2 says nothing about the blind, instead focusing on the poor, the brokenhearted, the captives, those who are bound. A close reading of Jesus's wording has caused some scholars to believe that he was adding Isaiah 42:7 to his reading, as a kind of commentary.[2] *This* prophecy says that the mission of God's coming "servant" is "to open the eyes that are blind, to bring out the prisoners from the dungeon, from the prison those who sit in darkness." Thus Jesus has in mind those who are imprisoned in spiritual darkness too.[3]

The response of his fellow Jews, initially favorable, quickly turns ugly. Knowing his humble roots, they question his authority. Jesus responds by strongly implying that they are faithlessly rejecting him: "Truly, I say to you, no prophet is acceptable in his hometown" (Luke 4:24). They get the hint and prove him right: "When they heard these things, all in the synagogue were filled with wrath. And they rose up and drove him out of the town and brought him to the brow of the hill on which their town was built, so that they could throw him down the cliff" (vv. 28–29).

They want neither Christ's liberty nor his light. At the very beginning, rejection becomes a hallmark of Christ's earthly ministry. As Isaiah himself said, "Who has believed our message?" (Isa. 53:1 NASB).

Later, after Jesus's ministry has been established, even John the Baptist, the new Elijah sent to prepare the way,[4] struggles to understand Christ and his mission (see Luke 7:18–23). "Are you the one who is to come," an imprisoned John asks through his own disciples, "or shall we look for another?" (Matt. 11:3). In reply, Jesus takes him back to Isaiah's prophecies: "The blind receive their sight and the lame walk, lepers are cleansed and the deaf hear, and the dead are raised up, and the poor have good news preached to them" (v. 5).

These are the very things Jesus has been doing in his public ministry. The Lord opens both physical *and* spiritual eyes. Those oppressed by disease and disability receive their freedom, as do those oppressed by sin. Jesus's earthly ministry illustrates and authenticates his spiritual ministry.

APPLICATION

**Physical and spiritual ministry
belong together.**

40

"Zeal for Your House Will Consume Me"

Psalm 69:9; John 2:14–17

Zeal is defined as "eagerness and ardent interest in pursuit of something."[1] Though it is an old-fashioned–sounding word, we see people display zeal in everything from their hobbies to their careers. Think, for example, about the passion expressed for a favorite college or professional sports team. About the only area of modern life where zeal is frowned on is in religion, where it is labeled "fanaticism," and scenes from the Salem witch trials or the Crusades are duly replayed.

Yet few would disparage someone who shows zeal for his *love*. This is what Jesus shows at the beginning of his ministry one Passover[2] at the temple in Jerusalem.

> In the temple he found those who were selling oxen and sheep and pigeons, and the money-changers sitting there. And making a whip of cords, he drove them all out of the temple, with the sheep and oxen. And he poured out the coins of the money-changers and overturned their tables. And he told those who sold the pigeons, "Take these things away; do not make my Father's house a house of trade." His disciples remembered that it was written, "Zeal for your house will consume me."
>
> John 2:14–17

The quotation is from Psalm 69:9, penned a thousand years before by David, who proposed the building of the temple in Jerusalem and gave much of his substance for its completion. In fact zealous worship of God was a lifelong pattern for David, who drew the reproach of his wife, Michal, when, leaping and dancing, he zealously brought the ark of the covenant to Jerusalem (2 Sam. 6:16).

Such zeal for the things of God will often upset the religious applecart. But it is exceedingly rare in our day, which tolerates religion as long as it remains "personal" and "private" and does not intrude on the secular consensus.

Tim Tebow, who is as well-known for his bold faith as he is for his football exploits, has ruffled more than a few feathers in his brief NFL career. Former Broncos quarterback Jake Plummer said that he wished Tebow would not talk about his religion all the time. Tebow responded that he would praise the Lord at every opportunity, saying it is like a man who declares his love for his wife.[3]

Tebow's commendable zeal for the Lord has drawn the ire of many. As David said in the second half of the verse, "The reproaches of those who reproach you have fallen on me." Jesus certainly understood that kind of reaction, for he faced it himself—from the religious leaders of his day, no less (see John 2:18–22). Upset by his zeal for the Lord, they demanded proof of his authority—skipping over the obvious fact that the corrupted temple *needed* to be cleansed.

In answer, Jesus announced a prophecy of his own: "Destroy this temple, and in three days I will raise it up" (v. 19).[4]

APPLICATION

Does your zeal for God offend others?

41

Miracle Worker

Isaiah 35:4–6

In John 9[1] Jesus sees a man who was born blind. "Rabbi," the disciples ask him, "who sinned, this man or his parents, that he was born blind?" Jesus tells them their focus is off, as if they are looking through the wrong end of a telescope, saying, "It was not that this man sinned, or his parents, but that the works of God might be displayed in him." Then Jesus sets about displaying those works, mixing some mud with his own spit and rubbing the concoction on the eyes of the blind beggar, whom he tells to go wash. The man "went and washed and came back seeing"—setting off a firestorm of doubt and controversy.

The man's neighbors and those who have regularly seen him begging can scarcely believe that a miracle has occurred. Some ask, "Is this not the man who used to sit and beg?" Some onlookers say, "It is he." Others, however, reply, "No, but he is like him." They forget to ask the man himself, who keeps on saying, "I am the man." Those with disabilities are often treated as nonentities.

Soon some Jewish leaders arrive, and they, too, are incredulous about Jesus performing the miracle (primarily because it has taken place on the Sabbath, which makes it, in their minds, forbidden work). To the man who was born blind, they say, "Give glory to God. We know that [Jesus] is a sinner."

This is too much for the former beggar, who answers acidly, "Why, this is an amazing thing! . . . Never since the world began has it been heard that anyone opened the eyes of a man born blind. If this man were not from God, he could do nothing."

Skeptics of the Bible often dismiss it as a collection of fairy tales and fables from an age when gullible people were quick to claim that anything they didn't understand—from the sun rising and setting to the vagaries of the weather—was a miracle. But a close reading of the New Testament belies this claim. The formerly blind man said that "never since the world began" was anyone who was born blind actually healed. Joseph doubted Mary's story of a miraculous conception. The disciples, for their part, basically ignored Jesus's repeated predictions of his coming resurrection and doubted when it happened because it did not compute with their expectations.

The Old Testament prophets, however, insisted that *miracles* would accompany the coming Messiah.

> Say to those who have an anxious heart,
>   "Be strong; fear not!
> Behold, your God
>   will come with vengeance,
> with the recompense of God.
>   He will come and save you."
> Then the eyes of the blind shall be opened,
>   and the ears of the deaf unstopped;
> then shall the lame man leap like a deer,
>   and the tongue of the mute sing for joy.
>   Isaiah 35:4–6

Anyone with even a passing knowledge of Jesus of Nazareth knows of his reputation for miracles—compassionately changing water into wine; healing the lame, blind, deaf, and mute; casting out demons; and raising the dead. His miracles were indisputable, and many people followed him around in hopes of receiving one.

Yet Jesus was concerned that people see beyond the immediate benefits of his miracles to their ultimate significance. Many, however, could not, or would not, connect the dots. "Though he had done so many signs before them, they still did not believe in him" (John 12:37). Then, as now, miracles are a tough sell to a skeptical heart.

APPLICATION

What would it take for you to really believe in Jesus?

42

"God Will Raise Up a Prophet Like Me from among Your Brothers"

Deuteronomy 18:15; John 5:46; Acts 3:22–26

Imagining Judaism without Moses is kind of like making a milkshake without milk—absurd and self-contradicting. Without Moses, Abraham's progeny would still be slaves in Egypt, and the law would never have been given at Sinai. "Along with God, it is the figure of Moses (*Moshe*) who dominates the Torah," Joseph Telushkin asserts. "Acting at God's behest, it is he who leads the Jews out of slavery, unleashes the Ten Plagues against Egypt, guides the freed slaves for forty years in the wilderness, carries down the law from Mount Sinai, and prepares the Jews to enter the land of Canaan."[1]

Moses is perhaps *the* towering figure in all of ancient history, revered by Jews, Christians, and Muslims the world over. Images of Moses—as portrayed by Michelangelo, Charlton Heston, and Tintoretto—stride across our collective mental landscape and grace the Supreme Court building. Deuteronomy 34:10 says, "And there has not arisen a prophet since in Israel like Moses, whom the LORD knew face to face," and most of us would agree that there will never be another Moses.

However, Moses himself disagreed. "The LORD your God will raise up for you a prophet like me from among you, from your brothers—it is to him you shall listen," he said (Deut. 18:15). This prophecy is given in the context of his warnings to the people of God not to take up pagan practices such as divination and necromancy. On one level, Moses is simply telling the people that the Lord will raise up other prophets to guide them. And certainly men such as Samuel, Nathan, Elijah, Elisha, Micah, and Nahum were called by God to announce his program at critical junctures in Israel's history—telling forth his will and foretelling the future.[2]

Yet the singular nature of this prophecy of Moses excited in the Jewish people an expectation of something—or, better yet, Someone—to come. It was easy for many to see the wonderworking Jesus in this role. As John 6:14 relates, "When the people saw the sign that he had done, they said, 'This is indeed the Prophet who is to come into the world!'"

More than miracles were involved, however. In his Sermon on the Mount (Matthew 5–7), Jesus was on a *new* mountain, authoritatively interpreting Mosaic law: "You have heard it said . . . but *I* say unto you. . . ." Jesus was the *new* Lawgiver, explaining the inner, spiritual requirements of the Torah. Jesus himself made the connection, saying to his Jewish listeners, "For if you believed Moses, you would believe me; for he wrote of me" (John 5:46).

The nascent church, which was constituted mostly of Jews, *did* believe. In one of his earliest sermons, the apostle Peter proclaimed:

> Moses said, "The Lord God will raise up for you a prophet like me from your brothers. You shall listen to him in whatever he tells you. And it shall be that every soul who does not listen to that prophet shall be destroyed from the people." And all the prophets who have spoken, from Samuel and those who came after him, also proclaimed these days. You are the sons of the prophets and of the covenant that God made with your fathers, saying to Abraham, "And in your offspring shall all the families of the earth be blessed." God, having raised up his servant, sent him to you first, to bless you by turning every one of you from your wickedness.
>
> Acts 3:22–26

APPLICATION

Jesus perfectly explains—and fulfills—the Law of God.

43

The Cornerstone

Psalm 118:22–23; Matthew 21:33–44

The saying "One man's trash is another man's treasure" illustrates perfectly what sometimes happens on *Antiques Roadshow*, a popular, long-running television program. Typically a guest will bring in an old item sold as junk for a few dollars at an estate sale. The appraiser will look it over, explain its provenance and condition, and tell the new owner that the item is really worth thousands—perhaps *tens* of thousands—of dollars. The original owner, seeing all this unfold on TV, would certainly experience a profound sense of loss and regret.

That's the idea behind Psalm 118:22–23: "The stone that the builders rejected has become the cornerstone. This is the LORD's doing; it is marvelous in our eyes." According to *Barnes' Notes on the Bible*, "a stone regarded as unfit to be worked into any part of a building, might be in reality so important that it would be laid yet at the very corner, and become the most valuable stone in the edifice—that on which the whole superstructure would rest."[1]

The context of Psalm 118 reinforces this point. It tells of the writer's trust in the Lord amid human opposition and of his ultimate vindication from God. As verses 5 and 6 say: "Out of my distress I called on the LORD; the LORD answered me and set me free. The LORD is on my side; I will not fear. What can man do to me?"

The Jewish people, of course, saw in this psalm a picture of their dealings with the larger world: "the imperial powers had thought little of

Israel, but God had chosen his people to be the cornerstone of his great plan for the world."[2] Some Jewish commentators took it further, seeing a hint of the coming Messiah.[3] Jesus agreed with them.

Toward the end of Jesus's ministry, he tells the parable of the tenants, who were responsible for the master's vineyard (Matt. 21:33–41). The parable outlines the historical rejection of the Old Testament prophets, who sought to revive the people's faithfulness to God. In the parable, the tenants abuse and kill one servant of the master after another. Finally, the story culminates with the tenants' rejection and murder of the owner's own son.

The parable, of course, is a warning to the Jewish leaders of the day, who are rejecting God's messenger as their forefathers had done. To drive home the point, Jesus quotes from their own Scriptures:

Jesus said to them, "Have you never read in the Scriptures:

> 'The stone that the builders rejected
>   has become the cornerstone;
> this was the Lord's doing,
>   and it is marvelous in our eyes'?

"Therefore I tell you, the kingdom of God will be taken away from you and given to a people producing its fruits. And the one who falls on this stone will be broken to pieces; and when it falls on anyone, it will crush him."

Matthew 21:42–44

Jesus says that *he* is the rejected cornerstone, the treasure thought to be trash. While this Prophet will indeed be killed, it is the unfaithful Jewish leaders who face ultimate loss and regret. But this is in no way a rejection of the Jewish people, who fulfill Abraham's prophecy to bless the nations,[4] helping to establish a new temple for God, consisting of both Jew and Gentile, with "Christ Jesus himself being the cornerstone" (Eph. 2:20).

APPLICATION

**Human rejection does not invalidate
God's calling.**

44

Riding a Donkey

Zechariah 9:9; Matthew 21:1–11

After the Roman commander Titus had crushed the Jewish rebellion and destroyed the second temple in AD 70, Emperor Vespasian held a triumphal procession for his son in Rome. The Jewish historian Josephus describes the scene:

> Vespasian and Titus came out crowned with laurel, and clothed in those ancient purple habits which were proper to their family. . . . Now a tribunal had been erected before the cloisters, and ivory chairs had been set upon it, when they came and sat down upon them. Whereupon the soldiery made an acclamation of joy to them immediately, and all gave them attestations of their valor. . . . When they had put on their triumphal garments, and had offered sacrifices to the gods that were placed at the gate, they sent the triumph forward, and marched through the theatres, that they might be the more easily seen by the multitudes.[1]

Not four decades before, Jerusalem had been the scene of another procession, this one of an entirely different character.

> Now when they drew near to Jerusalem and came to Bethphage, to the Mount of Olives, then Jesus sent two disciples, saying to them, "Go into the village in front of you, and immediately you will find a donkey tied, and a colt with her. Untie them and bring them to me. If anyone says anything to you, you shall say, 'The Lord needs them,' and he will send them at once."
>   . . . The disciples went and did as Jesus had directed them. They brought the donkey and the colt and put on them their cloaks, and he

sat on them. Most of the crowd spread their cloaks on the road, and others cut branches from the trees and spread them on the road. And the crowds that went before him and that followed him were shouting, "Hosanna to the Son of David! Blessed is he who comes in the name of the Lord! Hosanna in the highest!" And when he entered Jerusalem, the whole city was stirred up, saying, "Who is this?" And the crowds said, "This is the prophet Jesus, from Nazareth of Galilee."

Matthew 21:1–3, 6–11

A king riding on a donkey? The contrast between the usual military pomp for the man who destroyed Jerusalem and the procession outside Jerusalem for the humble Son of David is striking. Yet the people at Jerusalem go along, as if they were expecting it. Actually, they were. The postexilic prophet Zechariah had seen this event half a millennium before.

> Rejoice greatly, O daughter of Zion!
>   Shout aloud, O daughter of Jerusalem!
> Behold, your king is coming to you;
>   righteous and having salvation is he,
> humble and mounted on a donkey,
>   on a colt, the foal of a donkey.
>
> Zechariah 9:9

While other leaders marched in with armies or were mounted on impressive steeds, Jesus rides into the city on a donkey, a beast of burden "used by those who were traveling peaceably."[2] Instead of displaying the spoils taken from conquered enemies, he comes with his own gift—salvation. In fact, when this king comes, the end of warfare, though far in the future, is nevertheless in sight—and not just for Israel but for the world. Isaiah 9:6 predicts a coming "Prince of Peace." As Zechariah prophesied, "He shall speak peace to the nations; his rule shall be from sea to sea, and from the River to the ends of the earth" (Zech. 9:10).

Yet those in Jerusalem who did not welcome his peaceable rule would one day face God's wrath—starting with the destruction wrought by Titus.

APPLICATION

**Take the Lord's offer of peace
while it is available.**

Jesus—Death and Resurrection

45

"The Son of Man Will Suffer, Be Rejected, Be Killed, and Rise Again in Three Days"

Mark 8:31–33

In first-century Israel nearly everyone was looking for the Messiah, who was expected to deliver the people militarily from the hated Roman oppressors. Then Jesus comes on the scene, feeding the hungry and opening the reluctant eyes of a blind man through patient ministry (Mark 8:1–26).

Then a Pharisee interrogation team arrives, demanding a sign from this religious upstart. After already performing one miracle after another, Jesus simply answers, "Why does this generation seek a sign? Truly, I say to you, no sign will be given to this generation" (v. 12). Tangible proof of his identity is not enough, so they will get nothing more. Yet Jesus is very interested in what his *followers* think:

> And on the way he asked his disciples, "Who do people say that I am?" And they told him, "John the Baptist; and others say, Elijah; and others, one of the prophets." And he asked them, "But who do you say that I am?" Peter answered him, "You are the Christ." And he strictly charged them to tell no one about him.
>
> verses 27–30

Peter, the impulsive apostle, unlike Jesus's many critics, confesses the truth. But like most of his contemporaries, Peter thinks the Messiah's main job is to restore Israel's national greatness. Like the blind man who needed extra attention from Jesus to receive the full cure, Peter's vision remains cloudy. So Jesus begins to set him straight: "And [Jesus] began to teach them that the Son of Man must suffer many things and be rejected by the elders and the chief priests and the scribes and be killed, and after three days rise again. And he said this plainly" (vv. 31–32a).

This plan doesn't make sense to Peter, however. Only victories are supposed to be possible for the Messiah (and his followers). "And Peter took him aside and began to rebuke him. But turning and seeing his disciples, he rebuked Peter and said, 'Get behind me, Satan! For you are not setting your mind on the things of God, but on the things of man'" (vv. 32b–33).

Jesus says his ultimate victory will be attained only after his rejection by the Jewish leaders. Any other plan, however desirable on the surface, is a "thing of man," inspired by Satan. The Christ must die before he is raised.

So does Peter wait patiently for Christ's prophecy of the coming resurrection to be fulfilled? No, as the forces of darkness close in, Peter abandons his Lord and goes into hiding. Seeing his dreams unravel, Peter, like the skeptics before him, now needs proof about Jesus.

And in fulfilling the prophecy, the Lord graciously gives it to him.

On Friday Jesus is crucified between two thieves and, as another prophecy predicted (see Isa. 53:9; Matt. 27:57–60), laid to rest in a rich man's tomb. The following Sunday two faithful women (not Peter) come to the tomb, find that Jesus's body is gone, and see an angel with a startling message. "Do not be alarmed," the messenger says. "You seek Jesus of Nazareth, who was crucified. He has risen; he is not here. See the place where they laid him. But go, tell his disciples and Peter that he is going before you to Galilee. There you will see him, just as he told you" (Mark 16:6–7).

"Tell Peter." In the midst of doubt, grace; in the midst of despair, life from the dead. Often the "things of God" make sense only after the fact.

APPLICATION

Sometimes we must wait patiently in the darkness for the Lord's light to come.

46

The Sign of Jonah
Matthew 12:22–41

Jonah is the *reluctant* prophet. Knowing God's merciful heart, he goes
AWOL when the Lord sends him with a word of judgment to Israel's
enemies. Jonah jumps on a ship bound for faraway Tarshish, but the crew
throws him overboard, and the Lord sends a giant fish to pluck him from
the sea. After three days in the belly of the creature, Jonah is vomited
onto dry land. Chastened, the prophet goes to Nineveh and delivers God's
warning. No flashy miracles occur. Nevertheless the evil Assyrians repent
and are spared—much to Jonah's consternation.[1]

Centuries later other hardhearted Israelites are in God's sights. Jesus
of Nazareth has come preaching good news, healing the sick, and casting
out demons. Yet members of the religious intelligentsia, their preeminent
positions threatened, comb through the evidence, looking for something
with which to discredit him. First, they dismiss his miracles, saying (oddly)
that they have been done on God's holy day and thus cannot be of God.
Second, they say that any miracle of Jesus must have been done "by
Beelzebul, the prince of demons" (Matt. 12:24).

Warned by Jesus that they have reached the point of no return (vv.
22–37), and after rejecting all of his previous miracles, they nonetheless
ask for a sign—perhaps hoping that Jesus will fail in the clutch. The
Lord, however, is unwilling to play along.

> But he answered them, "An evil and adulterous generation seeks for
> a sign, but no sign will be given to it except the sign of the prophet
> Jonah. For just as Jonah was three days and three nights in the belly

of the great fish, so will the Son of Man be three days and three nights in the heart of the earth. The men of Nineveh will rise up at the judgment with this generation and condemn it, for they repented at the preaching of Jonah, and behold, something greater than Jonah is here."

verses 39–41

The time for miracles is past; now is the time for a decision. Jesus's opponents have had more than enough evidence—more, in fact, than had the evil Ninevites. Instead of receiving the role of Jonah the messenger, they are compared with the Ninevites, who, stunningly, excel them in faith. While these pagans repented at the mere preaching of judgment, those who were supposed to represent God on earth have rejected the miracles performed right in front of their eyes.

Unbelief is never due to a lack of evidence but to a lack of faith, which is the gift of God (Eph. 2:8). They *cannot* see because they *will* not see. So all they will get henceforward is "the sign of Jonah." Just as Jonah was "buried" in the heart of the sea, so Jesus will be buried in the heart of the earth. Jonah's "burial" was a sign of both judgment and grace, a precursor to what is about to happen in Jerusalem. The Lord's coming death and resurrection are signs of God's judgment against sin and grace for those who respond in faith.

The men of Nineveh repented at the preaching of Jonah, but the men of Jerusalem have hardened their hearts against "something greater than Jonah." So Jesus's final miracle—his death, burial, and resurrection three days later—is the ultimate sign to these skeptics standing at the rim of hell.

Will they be saved? Jesus is not holding his breath: "If they do not hear Moses and the Prophets, neither will they be convinced if someone should rise from the dead" (Luke 16:31).

APPLICATION

**Take advantage of God's grace before
you face his judgment.**

47

Betrayed

Psalm 41:9; John 13:18

Treachery, the unexpected betrayal of trust, has a long pedigree in human history. Cain took his brother, Abel, who offered a better sacrifice, into a lonely field and there slew him. Brutus assassinated Caesar, who said in surprise as the knife sank into his back, "*Et tu, Brute?*" Benedict Arnold turned on George Washington, who had decorated him as a war hero, before fleeing across the Atlantic. American John Walker Lindh attended some lectures by Osama bin Laden before 9/11, participated with the Taliban in attacks against U.S. forces, and was finally captured after a bloody prison uprising in Afghanistan.

All these men and many more rightly earned the ugly title of "traitor"—but excelling them all was Judas Iscariot, the disciple who betrayed Jesus for a mere thirty pieces of silver (in fulfillment of Zechariah 11:12). Judas is the name that will live forever in infamy. Dante consigns Judas to the lowest circle of hell, his head stuffed into the center of Satan's icy maw, to be chewed on forever.

Before Judas, however, there was Ahithophel, the trusted confidant and advisor of King David. Great leaders surround themselves with great men, and Ahithophel was nothing if not great in wisdom. According to God's Word, "Now in those days the counsel that Ahithophel gave was as if one consulted the word of God; so was all the counsel of Ahithophel esteemed" (2 Sam. 16:23).

Familiarity can breed contempt, however, and Ahithophel, like all traitors, decides that a new agenda trumps old-fashioned fidelity. David's young and handsome son, Absalom, is attempting to wrest the throne from his aging, discredited father, whose aura of invincibility has long since worn off. For Ahithophel, Absalom seems like the better bet, and so he joins the conspiracy—and the results are devastating for David, who has lost not only his son but his trusted counselor. Many commentators believe that David had Ahithophel in mind when he wrote Psalm 41:9: "Even my close friend in whom I trusted, who ate my bread, has lifted his heel against me."

David seems to be saying that Ahithophel is standing over him when he is down and defenseless, ready to stomp without mercy. Imagine the pain—physical, emotional, and spiritual.

Now fast-forward nearly one thousand years to the Last Supper. The whips, the crown of thorns, and the cross loom within hours as the merciless opponents of Jesus close in for the kill. But during the meal, Jesus is giving final instructions to the Twelve. The Lord has just done the unimaginable. He has removed his outer clothing, wrapped a towel around his waist like a slave, and washed the disciples' feet, including those of Judas. It is an object lesson for what they are to do in his absence—love and serve one another.

To make sure they don't miss the point, Jesus says, "Truly, truly, I say to you, a servant is not greater than his master, nor is a messenger greater than the one who sent him. If you know these things, blessed are you if you do them" (John 13:16–17). Yet Jesus is not quite finished, adding ominously: "I am not speaking of all of you; I know whom I have chosen. But the Scripture will be fulfilled, 'He who ate my bread has lifted his heel against me'" (v. 18).

Judas, unnamed at this point, is excluded from the blessed people of God, just as Ahithophel was. The Scripture ties the two traitors with unbreakable bonds. In fact, when Judas's treachery is discovered, like Ahithophel, he goes out and hangs himself (see 2 Sam. 17:23 and Matt. 27:5).

APPLICATION

**Decisions made in a moment can have
eternal consequences.**

48

"Strike the Shepherd and the Sheep Will Be Scattered"

Zechariah 13:7; Matthew 26:31

Great leaders inspire great devotion and risk-taking in their followers. Whether in sports, politics, business, or war, a leader gets others to buy in to his vision. Selfishness disappears, replaced by an *esprit de corps* that one cannot fully comprehend except from the inside. Winston Churchill, for example, had this effect on the British people in the Second World War. On May 13, 1940, the new prime minister stood before the House of Commons and issued a stirring call to arms against Nazi Germany:

> You ask, what is our policy? I will say: It is to wage war, by sea, land and air, with all our might and with all the strength that God can give us; to wage war against a monstrous tyranny, never surpassed in the dark and lamentable catalogue of human crime. That is our policy. You ask, what is our aim? I can answer in one word: victory; victory at all costs, victory in spite of all terror, victory, however long and hard the road may be; for without victory, there is no survival.[1]

Such leadership in the face of danger and desperation carried the Allies to victory. It is a small taste of the kind of leadership Jesus exercised during his earthly ministry. Jesus confounded his skeptics, thrilled the crowds, healed the sick, sent the demons running, and emboldened his disciples to spread an unstoppable kingdom. With Jesus leading the way, the sky was the limit.

With Jesus's followers multiplying, his opponents can only exclaim in frustration, "Look, the world has gone after him" (John 12:19). To keep the Roman tyrants from marching in against the one these leaders believe is a rival king, they think they must stop him. Unfortunately for them, they have lost the argument. They cannot convince the people, who are beginning to see Jesus as the long-awaited Messiah. But the enemies of Jesus believe they can stop the movement anyway—by murder. As the high priest says, "It is better for you that one man should die for the people, not that the whole nation should perish" (11:50).

After the Last Supper, Judas has exited to put their plan in motion. Jesus is warning the disciples who remain that the coming events will be more bitter than they can imagine. "You will all fall away because of me this night. For it is written, 'I will strike the shepherd, and the sheep of the flock will be scattered'" (Matt. 26:31).

Jesus is quoting Zechariah 13:7. Zechariah is the prophet who also predicted that Jesus would ride into Jerusalem on a donkey.[2] The disciples' supposedly unshakable devotion is about to be found wanting. *All* will flee like sheep when their shepherd leader is attacked. They will give up. As others would wistfully say only a few days later, "But we had hoped that he was the one to redeem Israel" (Luke 24:21). Humanly speaking, hope is gone.

And indeed, that very night, all these disillusioned and fearful men will desert their Lord, leaving him to face his fate alone. Yet Jesus leaves them with hope: "But after I am raised up, I will go before you to Galilee" (Matt. 26:32).

They have abandoned their leader, but he, the Good Shepherd, will never abandon his sheep. Zechariah also foresees an ultimate reconciliation: "They will call upon my name, and I will answer them. I will say, 'They are my people'; and they will say, 'The LORD is my God'" (Zech. 13:9).

APPLICATION

Great leaders don't stop leading, even when their followers stop following.

49

"You Will Deny Me Three Times"

Mark 14:29–31, 66–72

Simon, a rough and ready fisherman, was first among equals as one of the apostles. When Jesus first sized him up, he changed his name to Peter, meaning "Rock" (John 1:42). You would love Peter as a teammate but fear him as an opponent. If Peter was on board, he was "all in."

Peter is the one with the faith to go to his Lord on the water. It is Peter who seeks explanations from Jesus about his parables and his teaching on forgiveness. The temple tax collectors go to Peter for payment. Peter speaks up for the disciples and is a member of Jesus's inner circle. It is Peter who identifies Jesus as the Christ, the Son of the living God. After this remarkable confession of faith, Jesus selects Peter to lead the early church.[1]

But tonight Jesus is leading his disciples to the Garden of Gethsemane, telling them that the path leads to the cross. Though he has tried to break this horrible news before, they were never able to absorb it. Now, however, the awful truth is starting to settle in. Crucifixion, practiced by the Romans as a means of both torture and terror, is a particularly fiendish and humiliating form of execution, especially for a Jew. As Deuteronomy 21:23 says, "A hanged man is cursed by God."

Then Jesus adds insult to injury, predicting his men's imminent desertion. Peter—the strong, sword-carrying leader—will have none of this prophecy, at least for himself. "Peter said to him, 'Even though they all fall away, I will not.' And Jesus said to him, 'Truly, I tell you, this very night, before the rooster crows twice, you will deny me three times.' But he said emphatically, 'If I must die with you I will not deny you'" (Mark 14:29–31).

Surely Peter has the earlier statement of Jesus ringing in his ears: "So everyone who acknowledges me before men, I also will acknowledge before my Father who is in heaven, but whoever denies me before men, I also will deny before my Father who is in heaven" (Matt. 10:32–33). This is not just a matter of pride for Peter, but of eternal destiny.

And he fails just the same. Jesus is taken away, and Peter, ever the bold one, follows, but at a discreet distance.

> And as Peter was below in the courtyard, one of the servant girls . . . said, "You also were with the Nazarene, Jesus." But he denied it, saying, "I neither know nor understand what you mean." And . . . the rooster crowed. And the servant girl . . . began again to say to the bystanders, "This man is one of them." But again he denied it. And after a little while the bystanders again said to Peter, "Certainly you are one of them, for you are a Galilean." But he began to invoke a curse on himself and to swear, "I do not know this man of whom you speak." And immediately the rooster crowed a second time. And Peter remembered how Jesus had said to him, "Before the rooster crows twice, you will deny me three times." And he broke down and wept.
>
> Mark 14:66–72

Yet this denial spells not the end for Peter but the beginning of the end of his self-reliance. He will need this perspective, as a key leader of the young church who will one day face his own crucifixion. Later a risen Jesus restores him both personally and in ministry (John 21:15–19), and Peter is never the same, no matter what.

APPLICATION

Put God-reliance above self-reliance.

50

"You Will Not Abandon My Soul to the Grave"

Psalm 16:10; Acts 2:22–32

In the twenty-first century everyone gets to go to heaven, if pop culture is to be believed. The ancient world, however, had few illusions. "Homer was hugely important in the world of late antiquity; and in Homer life after death is pretty bleak," scholar N. T. Wright says. "Whenever the question of bodily resurrection is raised in the ancient world the answer is negative."[1]

In some ways, the ancient Jewish view was similar. "The Hebrew *Sheol*, the place of the dead, is not very different from Homer's Hades," Wright notes. "People are asleep there. . . . That is the picture we get from most of the Old Testament."[2]

Yet in the progressive revelation of Scripture, we occasionally see glimmers of something more substantial awaiting us beyond the grave. Unlike the Greeks, the Jews' highest ideal is of *embodied life* on an earth originally created very good. So while most Jews focused on the here and now of life in the Promised Land as members of God's chosen people, the idea of resurrection emerged from time to time, echoing on the edge of perception like a minor key in a far-off grand symphony.

Job 19:27, Psalm 73, Daniel 12, and Isaiah 26:19[3] speak of resurrection as the reward of God for his people. There are accounts of some Old Testament figures, such as Enoch and Elijah, whose earthly lives were translated directly to life with God, bypassing death altogether.

Still, by the time of Jesus, the question is far from settled. The Pharisees, frequent opponents of the Lord and of the early church, believe in a physical resurrection to come. The Sadducees, who hold that only the five books of Moses are inspired, believe, much like modern atheists, that this life is all there is. The debate no doubt reflects a certain anxiety, even among Jews, "who through fear of death were subject to lifelong slavery" (Heb. 2:15). It is no wonder that, responding to that fear, Jesus counsels his listeners, "Do not fear those who kill the body but cannot kill the soul" (Matt. 10:28).

However, the disciple Peter, who had claimed he was ready to die with Jesus, flinched badly when the test came.[4] Yet mere weeks later, Peter is a lionhearted witness, preaching about Jesus's resurrection in Jerusalem. Undergirding the apostle's sudden boldness is a prophecy from David's Psalm 16. No longer afraid of the grave, Peter preaches:

God raised [Jesus] up, loosing the pangs of death, because it was not possible for him to be held by it. For David says concerning him,

"I saw the Lord always before me,
    for he is at my right hand that I may not be shaken;
therefore my heart was glad, and my tongue rejoiced;
    my flesh also will dwell in hope.
For you will not abandon my soul to Hades,
    or let your Holy One see corruption.
You have made known to me the paths of life;
    you will make me full of gladness with your presence."

Brothers, . . . David . . . both died and was buried, and his tomb is with us to this day. . . . He foresaw . . . the resurrection of the Christ, that he was not abandoned to Hades, nor did his flesh see corruption. This Jesus God raised up, and of that we all are witnesses.

Acts 2:24–32

Those who believe in Jesus no longer need to fear death. Right then, seeing Christ's resurrection as a fulfillment of David's ancient prophecy of life beyond the grave, thousands of fellow Jews also turn to the risen Christ in faith (vv. 37–41).

APPLICATION

**Christ's resurrection should give his
followers boldness in this life.**

51

Isaiah's Vision
Isaiah 53

A court official from Ethiopia is returning to his native land after a visit to Jerusalem to worship the Lord. The holy city has just been the scene of upheaval, with massive crowds, a string of ugly Roman crucifixions, and a curious teaching about a rabbi who supposedly rose from the dead. On the southern road to Gaza, and eventually Africa, the official stops his chariot, takes out a precious sacred scroll, and begins reading aloud about someone who is "like a sheep . . . led to the slaughter," wondering what it means.

But the pious man is not alone. The Spirit of God has placed nearby a Christian evangelist named Philip, who boldly asks the Ethiopian, "Do you understand what you are reading?"

"How can I," he replies, "unless someone guides me?" So the evangelist joins the Ethiopian, who quickly asks a second question: "About whom, I ask you, does the prophet say this, about himself or about someone else?"

"Then Philip opened his mouth, and beginning with this Scripture he told him the good news about Jesus." (See Acts 8:26–40 for the full account.) The passage the Ethiopian was reading is the fifty-third chapter of Isaiah, penned seven hundred years earlier. For the two millennia since this Sunday school lesson on the road to Gaza, many Christians have seen it as the premier messianic prophecy in the entire Bible for its clear predictions of the suffering, death, and resurrection of Jesus Christ. We will briefly examine here the fulfillment of this grand prophecy— Isaiah 53.

> Who has believed what he has heard from us?
>   And to whom has the arm of the LORD been revealed?
> For he grew up before him like a young plant,
>   and like a root out of dry ground;
> he had no form or majesty that we should look at him,
>   and no beauty that we should desire him.
> He was despised and rejected by men;
>   a man of sorrows, and acquainted with grief;
> and as one from whom men hide their faces
>   he was despised, and we esteemed him not.
> Surely he has borne our griefs
>   and carried our sorrows;
> yet we esteemed him stricken,
>   smitten by God, and afflicted.
>
> Isaiah 53:1–4

A Man of Sorrows. Jesus Christ was rejected by his people (John 1:11) and indeed by his own hometown, which saw him as merely the son of a nondescript carpenter (Luke 4:16–30). The religious leaders said he was a tool of the devil (Matt. 12:24). Before he was taken captive, Jesus's sweat was "like great drops of blood" (Luke 22:44). When put on trial, his accusers hit him, spit in his face, and snarled, "Prophesy to us, you Christ! Who is it that struck you?" (Matt. 26:68). As he hung on the cross, the mockery only intensified, with the rabble laughing. "He saved others; he cannot save himself" (27:42).

> But he was wounded for our transgressions;
>   he was crushed for our iniquities;
> upon him was the chastisement that brought us peace,
>   and with his wounds we are healed.
> All we like sheep have gone astray;
>   we have turned—every one—to his own way;
> and the LORD has laid on him
>   the iniquity of us all.
> He was oppressed, and he was afflicted,
>   yet he opened not his mouth;

> like a lamb that is led to the slaughter,
>> and like a sheep that before its shearers is silent,
>> so he opened not his mouth.
> By oppression and judgment he was taken away;
>> and as for his generation, who considered
> that he was cut off out of the land of the living,
>> stricken for the transgression of my people?
> And they made his grave with the wicked
>> and with a rich man in his death,
> although he had done no violence,
>> and there was no deceit in his mouth.

Isaiah 53:5–9

Punished for Others. Jesus, as Zechariah 12:10 also prophesies, was "pierced" in crucifixion—his hands, feet, and side punctured (see, for example, John 19:16–37)—yet said nothing in his own defense to the Sanhedrin (see, for example, John 18:19–24) or to Pontius Pilate (John 19:10). Jesus, who had no worldly goods except the clothes he wore, was placed in the tomb of a rich man (see Matt. 27:57–61; John 19:38–42). Jesus saw his death clearly as an atoning sacrifice for others, saying, "For even the Son of Man came not to be served but to serve, and to give his life as a ransom for many" (Mark 10:45).

> Yet it was the will of the LORD to crush him;
>> he has put him to grief;
> when his soul makes an offering for guilt,
>> he shall see his offspring; he shall prolong his days;
> the will of the LORD shall prosper in his hand.
> Out of the anguish of his soul he shall see and be satisfied;
> by his knowledge shall the righteous one, my servant,
>> make many to be accounted righteous,
>> and he shall bear their iniquities.
> Therefore I will divide him a portion with the many,
>> and he shall divide the spoil with the strong,
> because he poured out his soul to death
>> and was numbered with the transgressors;
> yet he bore the sin of many,
>> and makes intercession for the transgressors.

Isaiah 53:10–12

Raised to Life. Jesus, who died as a guilt offering for others, was raised to life again, as the unanimous witness of the early church claims (see, for example, Matt. 28:1–10). While others have denied it, a fair consideration of the evidence, including this prophecy, points to an actual physical resurrection. Acclaimed New Testament scholar N. T. Wright has said:

> [T]he historian may and must say that all other explanations for why Christianity arose, and why it took the shape it did, are far less convincing *as historical explanations* than the one the early Christians themselves offer: that Jesus really did rise from the dead on Easter morning, leaving an empty tomb behind him.[1]

After Philip finishes expounding the good news from Isaiah 53, the Ethiopian official is convinced that the passage is indeed about Jesus and that he needs to take on the sign of Christian discipleship. "See, here is water!" he exclaims. "What prevents me from being baptized?"

APPLICATION

**Have you allowed the evidence
for Christ's suffering, death,
and resurrection to change your life?**

52

The Seed versus the Serpent

Genesis 3:15

The United States is founded on the ideal of "life, liberty, and the pursuit of happiness." Rugged individualism and the cult of do-what-you-want are written into the American DNA. Americans believe they are equal both before the law and in the eyes of God. Conversely, we bristle at any suggestion that our individual fate is tied to anyone else's.

That's the reason we naturally balk at the biblical worldview that, yes, we *are* our brother's keeper. It's why we think it unfair that whole nations should face disaster or blessing because of the choices of their leaders (though this happens every day in the modern world). Isn't faith and goodness—or unbelief and badness—an individual choice?

Yet if we refuse to be tied to any notion of collective guilt, we wall ourselves off from the possibility of collective grace—and will face the consequences of our own sin utterly alone. Consider Adam and Eve's choice to listen to the serpent, which plunged the entire race into sin. If it is unfair for us to have to pay for their moral turpitude, then we will still have to pay for our own. But we will be paying without the benefit of a hopeful prophecy that God himself pronounced in the Garden of Eden. God tells the serpent: "I will put enmity between you and the woman, and between your offspring and her offspring; he shall bruise your head, and you shall bruise his heel" (Gen. 3:15).

The Lord speaks of enmity (or hatred) between the woman (Eve) and the serpent, and commentators down through the ages have seen a lot more going on here than mankind's primal fear of snakes. That's because the enmity will continue down through their offspring. It sounds very much like a *collective* conflict, doesn't it?

In this prophecy, God predicts the outcome: the head of the serpent will be bruised, but only the heel of the woman's offspring will be injured. The writers of the New Testament saw beyond the simple picture of a man stomping on a snake. They saw an ultimate Man dealing, at significant cost to himself, a death blow to the Prince of Darkness, "that through death he might destroy the one who has the power of death, that is, the devil, and deliver all those who through fear of death were subject to lifelong slavery" (Heb. 2:14–15).

Yes, Jesus Christ died on the cross but he was resurrected—breaking the power of Satan over a lost humanity. So while Jesus was bruised (figuratively), the devil's power—Revelation 20:2 identifies the serpent with the dragon, a.k.a. the devil—was crushed. As Paul said in Colossians 2:15, "[God] disarmed the rulers and authorities and put them to open shame, by triumphing over them in [Christ]." Yes, Christ's death on the cross served as the atoning sacrifice for our sins (1 John 2:2), but in a very real sense, it also broke the power of evil over humanity.

This is *collective grace*. Just as Adam, as the head (or "king") of the human race, plunged us all into spiritual slavery, so the "second Adam," the Lord Jesus, gave us access to spiritual freedom in God's family. But for those who still think this arrangement isn't fair, be advised that this collective grace must still be activated by *individual* choice. As John the apostle said, "But to all who did receive him, who believed in his name, he gave the right to become children of God" (John 1:12).

APPLICATION

**Have you received God's grace
for yourself?**

The Church

53

"Proclaimed throughout the Whole World"

Isaiah 42:6–7; 49:6; Matthew 24:14; Acts 1:6–8

Jesus has died and risen in Jerusalem. Any minute he will ascend to God the Father, but first he must impart some final instructions to the disciples (Acts 1:4–11). Israel's kingdom has been on hiatus since Nebuchadnezzar's brutal overthrow half a millennium ago, and the King, the new David, Jesus, has indeed arrived. Now he is exiting. Yet Rome still rules the Promised Land.

"Lord," the confused disciples ask, "will you at this time restore the kingdom to Israel?" Jesus's answer is neither a *yes* nor a *no*. It is instead a prophecy. "It is not for you to know times or seasons that the Father has fixed by his own authority. But you will receive power when the Holy Spirit has come upon you, and you will be my witnesses in Jerusalem and in all Judea and Samaria, and to the end of the earth" (vv. 6–8).

They are called not to prepare to occupy their thrones but to witness to their own people (in Jerusalem and Judea), to people of a similar culture and religion (the hated Samaritans), and to people of all cultures (to the ends of the earth). On their own, it is an impossibly big task, but one that will ultimately succeed because it reflects God's unstoppable concern for the nations.

Ever since the time of Abraham,[1] the Jewish people have known that they were blessed to be a global blessing. The prophet Isaiah saw Israel's worldwide obligation and opportunity more clearly than most. He spoke repeatedly of a coming Servant who would share God's glory not only with a repentant Israel but with a needy world.

> It is too light a thing that you should be my servant
>   to raise up the tribes of Jacob
>   and to bring back the preserved of Israel;
> I will make you as a light for the nations,
>   that my salvation may reach to the end of the earth.
>   Isaiah 49:6

> I am the LORD, . . .
> I will give you as a covenant for the people,
>   a light for the nations,
>   to open the eyes that are blind,
> to bring out the prisoners from the dungeon.
>   Isaiah 42:6–7

After twenty centuries of concentrated work with Israel to reveal and reflect who he is and to build a base of operations from which to launch a global rescue mission, God is shifting his concern for the world into overdrive. God's people, following the instructions of their Messiah, are now called to share their King with the nations, which are imprisoned and sitting in spiritual darkness.

And in the twenty centuries since the Spirit was poured out on Christ's handful of witnesses, Isaiah's and Christ's prophecies about the spread of the good news "throughout the whole world as a testimony to all nations" (Matt. 24:14) have been amazingly fulfilled. Christianity has become the world's largest and most global faith.

The Christian faith is increasingly centered outside the West, in Asia, Africa, and Latin America. Today, at the beginning of the twenty-first century, *Operation World* documents "the astonishing shift of Christianity's centre of gravity to the Majority World."[2] Missionaries by the thousands are pouring out of these formerly spiritually dark regions, spreading the light of Christ to peoples who have never heard of him—often working hand in hand with the Westerners who first brought the gospel to them.

APPLICATION

**The church shares Christ with the nations
in the power of the Spirit.**

54

The Outpouring
of the Spirit

Joel 2:28–29; Acts 2:2–4

Israel introduced the world's first great monotheistic faith. The Shema famously proclaims, "Hear, O Israel: The LORD our God, the LORD is one" (Deut. 6:4). It is Jehovah alone who is "the one absolute God, as King over all the earth."[1] Yet the language of the Hebrew Scriptures nudges our understanding past a bare monotheism, as in Islam, to a more complex view of what this one God is like. God, we learn, has (or is) a Spirit.

God's Spirit, we are told in the Old Testament, hovers over the waters at Creation; breathes life into mankind; temporarily lights upon God's specially chosen people, such as Samson or David, to accomplish his work in the world; and empowers God's representatives to prophesy. Yet for all this, the Spirit usually stays in the background of Israel's consciousness and daily life.

Then the prophet Joel appears, preaching a frightening message of judgment, of a "day of the Lord" that will be aimed not just at Israel's pagan enemies, but at the unrepentant people of God themselves. But the Lord is merciful, Joel says. The people's latter blessings will be greater than the former, because they will experience God's Spirit in a new way. The Spirit will be not just for the few, but for the many.

> And it shall come to pass afterward,
>> that I will pour out my Spirit on all flesh;

> your sons and your daughters shall prophesy,
>   your old men shall dream dreams,
>   and your young men shall see visions.
> Even on the male and female servants
>   in those days I will pour out my Spirit.
>
> Joel 2:28–29

This promise of the Spirit for the many seems almost too good to be true, and for hundreds of years, it also seems empty. Then John the Baptist comes along, saying about Jesus: "For he whom God has sent utters the words of God, for he gives the Spirit without measure" (John 3:34). Jesus in turn promises his followers that God the Father "will give you another Helper, to be with you forever, even the Spirit of truth" (14:16–17). The Spirit, the third Person of the Trinity, who has been confined to the few, and only for short times, will finally come to the many forever.

It happens in dramatic fashion. After Jesus's resurrection and ascension to heaven, the disciples are waiting together for the promised Helper.

> And suddenly there came from heaven a sound like a mighty rushing wind, and it filled the entire house where they were sitting. And divided tongues as of fire appeared to them and rested on each one of them. And they were all filled with the Holy Spirit and began to speak in other tongues as the Spirit gave them utterance.
>
> Acts 2:2–4

The Spirit, formerly in the background, has finally come roaring into the open, with power. Under the Helper's direction, a formerly fearful Peter boldly tells the wondering crowds that "this is what was uttered through the prophet Joel" (v. 16). Because of the Spirit, the world is forever turned "upside down" (17:6).

APPLICATION

**The Holy Spirit is available to
ALL of God's people.**

55

"I Will Build My Church"

Matthew 16:18

Jesus and his disciples have just entered the northern district of Caesarea Philippi. Jesus, who sometimes refers to himself by the enigmatic title, Son of Man,[1] asks his disciples, "Who do people say that the Son of Man is?" (See Matthew 16:13–20.) They describe a range of opinions: "Some say John the Baptist, others say Elijah, and others Jeremiah or one of the prophets."

"But who do you say that I am?"

Peter, as usual,[2] steps boldly forward with an answer: "You are the Christ, the Son of the living God." It is a brilliant theological insight for the fisherman, a monotheistic Jew, combining two exalted categories—the Christ (or Jewish Messiah) and the Son of God. It points to the paradoxical truth that Jesus is both human and divine.

"Blessed are you, Simon Bar-Jonah!" Jesus exclaims in response. "For flesh and blood has not revealed this to you, but my Father who is in heaven." Then Jesus follows up this statement with an encouraging prophecy: "And I tell you, you are Peter, and on this rock I will build my church, and the gates of hell shall not prevail against it."

Opposition is building against Jesus, the disciples have left everything to follow him, and the cross is already casting a dark shadow over their path. But Jesus is telling Peter, whose new name means "rock," that on him—or perhaps on his astounding, rock-solid confession of faith—he, Jesus, will build a church[3] that will never be destroyed. It is one thing, of course, to announce such an unlikely prediction, another to fulfill it. But history has borne out its accuracy.

Rome and the Jewish leadership, of course, collaborated to crucify Jesus, sending his followers into hiding. But the resurrection brought them roaring back. As the church of the Christ, the Son of the living God, spread, opponents—both Jewish and pagan—variously abused, martyred, and even ignored its members. Yet nothing worked, and Christ's followers spread across the ancient world.

Actually their biggest challenge may have come from within, initially from a heresy that denied the humanity of Christ. How one confessed Christ was indeed a foundation rock for the church. If the church becomes wobbly on either the deity or the humanity of Christ, then it crumbles like the proverbial house built on sand (see Matt. 7:24–27). One early heresy that shook the fledgling church was Arianism, which held that Christ was a created being rather than the eternal Son of God. This damnable doctrine was refuted at the First Council of Nicaea in AD 325.[4]

When the Roman Catholic Church fell into serious corruption and error, God raised up Reformers such as Luther and Calvin. When Islam drove Christians largely out of the Middle East and North Africa, the church experienced massive growth in the West. When the state-sponsored churches of Europe fell into decline, new communities of faith flowered in Asia, Africa, and Latin America—and in Europe itself. When atheistic Communism attempted to stamp out the church, it was the Communists themselves who were relegated to the ash heap of history.

Despite all the persecutions, heresies, and everything else that the gates of hell have contrived to throw at it, the church has prevailed. And it will continue to do so. Why? Because Christ has promised.

APPLICATION

Personal faith must include personal commitment to the church.

Last Days,
Second Advent,
and the
Final State

56

The Destruction of the Temple

Mark 13:1–2

Just as God covered the sin of Adam and Eve through the killing of an animal substitute and using the skins to clothe their nakedness (Gen. 3:21), so God told Moses to build a tabernacle so that a sinful people could relate to a holy God through an exacting system of animal sacrifice. As the Lord told his people, "I have given [blood] for you on the altar to make atonement for your souls, for it is the blood that makes atonement by the life" (Lev. 17:11).

The tabernacle, where the animals were sacrificed, was a vital but temporary structure to allow God to dwell with his people. A curtain barred access to the tabernacle's holiest section, where God's special presence dwelt.

Later David laid the groundwork for a magnificent temple in Jerusalem, built by Solomon. After the Babylonians destroyed this supposedly permanent structure, the Jews eventually built a smaller version that brought tears to the eyes of those who had seen the grander original (Ezra 3:12).

By the time of Christ, the evil Herod the Great was rebuilding the temple to a size twice that of its predecessor. Decked with marble and gold, it was 172 feet long, 172 feet wide, and 172 feet high.[1] Josephus said Herod made it "larger in compass, and to raise it to a most magnificent altitude, . . . for an everlasting memorial of him."[2]

Yet this temple would be, like its earlier versions, anything but everlasting. Just before his passion, Jesus pronounced its doom: "And as he came out of the temple, one of his disciples said to him, 'Look, Teacher, what wonderful stones and what wonderful buildings!' And Jesus said to him, 'Do you see these great buildings? There will not be left here one stone upon another that will not be thrown down'" (Mark 13:1–2).

Days later, when Christ died on the cross, the temple curtain was torn in two, from top to bottom, signifying that the barrier between God and man was now removed (Matt. 27:51). Though the law requiring blood for the remission of sin was never abrogated, the Jewish temple, with its perpetual sacrifices, was no longer necessary, because Christ's blood made a lasting and perfect sacrifice (see Heb. 10:1–12).

This was a precursor to the prophecy's ultimate fulfillment four decades later, with the destruction of Jerusalem and the temple wrought by Titus.[3] The Roman historian Tacitus said the general and others held this brutal act to be:

> a prime necessity in order to wipe out more completely the religion of the Jews and the Christians; for they urged that these religions, although hostile to each other, nevertheless sprang from the same sources; the Christians had grown out of the Jews: if the root were destroyed, the stock would easily perish.[4]

The loss of the temple and its sacrificial system was a cataclysmic event for Judaism, for "without the shedding of blood there is no forgiveness of sins" (Heb. 9:22). Bereft of the temple and yet unwilling, by and large, to receive Christ's sacrifice for themselves,[5] the Jewish people now look to the Talmud, a newer collection of oral tradition that interprets and applies the ancient Hebrew Scriptures in light of the loss of the sacrificial system.[6]

In the two millennia since its destruction, the temple has never been rebuilt. Only a lonely retaining wall built by Herod still stands.[7] On the Temple Mount now sits the Al-Aqsa Mosque, the third holiest site in Islam. The Jewish people couldn't rebuild the temple even if they wanted to.

Christians look to the temple as a temporary precursor to the free access to God they experience in Christ now, and which they will possess in full in the coming new Jerusalem. John the apostle said of that heavenly city, "And I saw no temple in the city, for its temple is the Lord God the Almighty and the Lamb" (Rev. 21:22).

APPLICATION

Christ's sacrifice renders the temple unnecessary.

57

The Second Coming

Mark 13:24–27; Acts 1:6–11

In C. S. Lewis's *The Last Battle*, Narnia's time is coming to an end, not with a naturalistic whimper but with a supernatural bang. An impossibly large giant blows a horn, and immediately the sky is filled with shooting stars, followed by an ominous starless patch. "The spreading blackness was not a cloud at all: it was simply emptiness. The black part of the sky was the part in which there were no stars left. All the stars were falling: Aslan had called them home."[1]

While many scientists are predicting that the universe in which we find ourselves will die of natural causes untold billions of years in the future, the Bible predicts without apology that the Creator will wrap things up suddenly and unmistakably. Yes, for millennia God has worked deliberately and patiently with Israel and the nations, for he "desires all people to be saved and to come to the knowledge of the truth" (1 Tim. 2:4). But this present era of opportunity is not endless.

Jesus has just told his disciples the unexpected prophecy that Herod's awesome temple will be thrown down, reduced to a pile of rubble.[2] Quite naturally, they want details, asking, "Tell us, when will these things be, and what will be the sign when all these things are about to be accomplished?" (Mark 13:4; see Mark 13 for the Olivet Discourse, from which the following quotes and observations come.)

Many Bible prophecies have an immediate fulfillment and a later, more complete fulfillment that often can be seen only in hindsight.[3] As

Jesus answers his disciples' questions on the Mount of Olives, we can see both dimensions of fulfilled prophecy. The temple was razed in AD 70, marking the end of the old Judaism. Hundreds of thousands of people died in the slaughter. First-century Christians, however, took seriously their Lord's command to flee to the mountains and escaped much of the devastation that engulfed their fellow Jews.

According to Josephus, "Through the roar of the flames streaming far and wide, the groans of the falling victims were heard; . . . the entire city seemed to be ablaze; and the noise—nothing more deafening and frightening could be imagined."[4]

But this calamity is only the beginning of the end, a foretaste of what is to come. After describing numerous signs of global distress, Jesus prophesies his eventual second coming:

> But in those days, after that tribulation, the sun will be darkened, and the moon will not give its light, and the stars will be falling from heaven, and the powers in the heavens will be shaken. And then they will see the Son of Man coming in clouds with great power and glory. And then he will send out the angels and gather his elect from the four winds, from the ends of the earth to the ends of heaven.
>
> Mark 13:24–27

But for now there is work to do. After giving his final instructions and encouragements to the disciples, Jesus ascends into heaven (see Acts 1:6–11). As the disciples stare, dumbfounded, two angels appear, saying: "Men of Galilee, why do you stand looking into heaven? This Jesus, who was taken up from you into heaven, will come in the same way as you saw him go into heaven" (v. 11).

Yes, the world as we know it will one day end, not with a whimper, but with a bang, as God's prophets have long predicted (see, for example, Zech. 14:1–9).

APPLICATION

Are you ready for the second coming of Christ?

No One Knows the Day or the Hour

Matthew 24:36

Radio broadcaster Harold Camping caused a stir in 2011 by predicting the date of the rapture—not once, but twice, on May 21 and October 21.[1] After the prophecies were proven to be false, Camping, 90, had a stroke,[2] retired from his ministry, and was "disappointed" that his predictions had failed.[3] Camping could have saved himself all the trouble and embarrassment if he had simply taken to heart what the New Testament says.

In chapter 53, "A Light for the Nations," we saw the disciples attempting to learn the date of Christ's return, and he tells them they have more important things to worry about—namely, the spread of the gospel. This is not the only place where our curiosity about setting a date is rebuffed. During his Olivet Discourse (see Mark 13 and Matthew 24), in answer to the disciples' question about the timing of his coming, Jesus gives some general signs of "great tribulation": persecutions, false Christs, wars, natural disasters, and awesome celestial portents. Then he tells his followers to be ready:

From the fig tree learn its lesson: as soon as its branch becomes tender and puts out its leaves, you know that summer is near. So also, when you see all these things, you know that he is near, at the very gates. Truly, I say to you, this generation will not pass away until all these things take place. Heaven and earth will pass away, but my words will not pass away.

Matthew 24:32–35

Bible scholars and students have wrestled with the meaning of this passage and the words "this generation." Some say that they refer to the people living when the time of the end begins. Others say that it refers to the people living at the time Jesus gave the prophecy, which, they say, primarily refers to the fall of Jerusalem in AD 70 by Titus. Jesus, however, doesn't provide the answer. "But concerning that day and hour no one knows, not even the angels of heaven, nor the Son, but the Father only" (v. 36).

Yet there are markers. For example, the apostle Paul told the church in Thessalonica that the end would not come "unless the rebellion comes first, and the man of lawlessness is revealed, the son of destruction, who opposes and exalts himself against every so-called god or object of worship, so that he takes his seat in the temple of God, proclaiming himself to be God" (2 Thess. 2:3–4).

Some commentators have identified the "son of destruction" as Titus; others, Emperor Caligula; others; the pope; and still others, a coming Antichrist who will focus Satan's opposition to God before the end. We cannot resolve this dispute here, but it is worth noting this statement from John the apostle: "Children, it is the last hour, and as you have heard that antichrist is coming, so now many antichrists have come. Therefore we know that it is the last hour" (1 John 2:18). Back in the first century John said that we are *already in* the last hour and that many antichrists have *already arrived*. We don't need to sit around speculating. *We are in the last days now.*

The important thing, Jesus says, is not precisely *when* these events will happen, but *what* we are doing when they do. "Therefore," he warns, "you also must be ready, for the Son of Man is coming at an hour you do not expect" (Matt. 24:44).

The apostle Peter, who was on hand for these sobering words, had the same perspective:

But do not overlook this one fact, beloved, that with the Lord one day is as a thousand years, and a thousand years as one day. The Lord is not slow to fulfill his promise as some count slowness, but is patient toward you, not wishing that any should perish, but that all should reach repentance. But the day of the Lord will come like a thief, and then the heavens will pass away with a roar, and the heavenly bodies will be burned up and dissolved, and the earth and the works that are done on it will be exposed.

Since all these things are thus to be dissolved, what sort of people ought you to be in lives of holiness and godliness, waiting for and hastening the coming of the day of God!

2 Peter 3:8–12

APPLICATION

**The key question regarding the second coming
is not when it will happen but what you
will be doing when it does.**

59

The Last Judgment

Matthew 25:31–46

Gracing the wall of the Sistine Chapel is Michelangelo's magnificent Renaissance fresco, *The Last Judgment*.[1] Angels blow their horns to raise the dead; one holds a book by which the dead are judged. Jesus stands in the center. Those on his right are escorted by angels to eternal bliss, while those on his left are brought to eternal destruction, escorted by Charon, the Greek god of the underworld. The finality of the scene is sobering, particularly in today's culture, in which nearly everyone feels entitled to endless second chances.

Yet the prophecies of the Bible converge to say that all of us will face a final day of reckoning. "Few truths are more often or more clearly proclaimed in Scripture than that of the general judgment," the *Catholic Encyclopedia* states. "To it the prophets of the Old Testament refer when they speak of the 'Day of the Lord' (Joel 2:31; Ezek. 13:5; Isa. 2:12), in which the nations will be summoned to judgment."[2]

Jesus's own prophecy of the last judgment is terrifying, as he no doubt intended:

> When the Son of Man comes in his glory, and all the angels with him, then he will sit on his glorious throne. Before him will be gathered all the nations, and he will separate people one from another as a shepherd separates the sheep from the goats. And he will place the sheep on his right, but the goats on the left. Then the King will say to those on his right, "Come, you who are blessed by my Father, inherit the kingdom

prepared for you from the foundation of the world. For I was hungry and you gave me food, I was thirsty and you gave me drink, I was a stranger and you welcomed me, I was naked and you clothed me, I was sick and you visited me, I was in prison and you came to me." Then the righteous will answer him, saying, "Lord, when did we see you hungry and feed you, or thirsty and give you drink? And when did we see you a stranger and welcome you, or naked and clothe you? And when did we see you sick or in prison and visit you?" And the King will answer them, "Truly, I say to you, as you did it to one of the least of these my brothers, you did it to me."

Then he will say to those on his left, "Depart from me, you cursed, into the eternal fire prepared for the devil and his angels. For I was hungry and you gave me no food, I was thirsty and you gave me no drink, I was a stranger and you did not welcome me, naked and you did not clothe me, sick and in prison and you did not visit me." Then they also will answer, saying, "Lord, when did we see you hungry or thirsty or a stranger or naked or sick or in prison, and did not minister to you?" Then he will answer them, saying, "Truly, I say to you, as you did not do it to one of the least of these, you did not do it to me." And these will go away into eternal punishment, but the righteous into eternal life.

Matthew 25:31–46

Both salvation and damnation, this prophecy teaches,[3] will be proven by our *works*—specifically, by acts of compassion done for Christ. How then do we square this teaching with our receiving God's forgiveness by faith based on Christ's death and resurrection on our behalf?[4] Is this a contradiction? No. The Bible teaches that salvation is by faith in Christ, not works (see, for example, Rom. 6:23), but that works will—and *must*—accompany any true faith (James 2:18). Faith in Christ's finished work on the cross is the ticket that will get us to heaven, but it is a ticket that also provides entrance to a life of good works. As Dietrich Bonhoeffer said, *"[O]nly he who believes is obedient, and only he who is obedient believes."*[5] So we are advised, before the books are opened, "Examine yourselves, to see whether you are in the faith" (2 Cor. 13:5).

APPLICATION

**How do you know if your name is
written in the "book of life"?[6]**

60

The New Heaven and the New Earth

Isaiah 65:17; Revelation 21:1–4

As we have seen in this volume, while the Bible presents an untold number of prophecies, they all converge in one overarching story:

> When Adam and Eve fall into sin, their loving Creator covers their shame with animal skins and promises a Redeemer who will one day crush the serpent's head.
>
> Four thousand years ago, God tells Abram that he will be blessed in order to bless the nations. Abraham's descendents become Israel, the vehicle of God's blessing. The Lord alternately blesses and disciplines the people of God and the nations around them, with a view to eventually reaching the entire world with his love and righteousness.
>
> The nation reaches a high point with King David before ultimately faltering, so God sends a new David, his Son Jesus Christ, to complete his plan to redeem Israel and the world by crushing the power of Satan.
>
> Christ, according to the plan of God, is rejected and crucified. After rising from the dead, Jesus sends his new community of faith, the church, to spread the Good News to Jew and Gentile alike until he returns as Judge, punishing the unrighteous and rewarding the faithful.

Now we have reached the end of this book, and the end of prophecy. For prophecy is, after all, merely a temporary light on the path toward our destination. "As for prophecies," the apostle Paul said, "they will pass away. . . . For we know in part and we prophesy in part, but when the perfect comes, the partial will pass away. . . . For now we see in a mirror dimly, but then face to face. Now I know in part; then I shall know fully, even as I have been fully known" (1 Cor. 13:8–9, 12).

Finally, the destination the prophets of both testaments have been pointing to is in sight. God will dwell with his people, no longer in a garden, but in a City, in a new universe, unstained by sin or sorrow.

> For behold, I create new heavens
>   and a new earth,
> and the former things shall not be remembered
>   or come into mind.
>
> Isaiah 65:17

Then I saw a new heaven and a new earth, for the first heaven and the first earth had passed away, and the sea was no more. And I saw the holy city, new Jerusalem, coming down out of heaven from God, prepared as a bride adorned for her husband. And I heard a loud voice from the throne saying, "Behold, the dwelling place of God is with man. He will dwell with them, and they will be his people, and God himself will be with them as their God. He will wipe away every tear from their eyes, and death shall be no more, neither shall there be mourning, nor crying, nor pain anymore, for the former things have passed away."

Revelation 21:1–4

Down through the centuries, Christians have disagreed—sometimes vehemently—about the particulars of this prophecy or that. Yet we have been united in our anticipation of the ultimate destination to which the prophecies so powerfully point us. "Beloved, we are God's children now, and what we will be has not yet appeared; but we know that when he appears we shall be like him, because we shall see him as he is" (1 John 3:2).

APPLICATION

The aim of all true prophecy is Jesus Christ.

Basic Principles and Resources for Interpreting the Bible

Background

Bible prophecy does not appear out of thin air. It is only one part, albeit an important one, of God's written Word, the Bible. We cannot expect to understand and apply Scripture's prophecies if we do not have a firm grasp of Scripture's principles. Failure to see this point has led to much misunderstanding and abuse of the Bible, including its prophecies.

The technical term for the science of interpreting the Bible is hermeneutics, derived from Hermes, the mythological messenger and interpreter of the gods.[1] We require proper hermeneutical principles and resources to accurately interpret the Bible, including its many prophecies.

While the Protestant Reformers, and Christians down through the succeeding centuries, have rightly held to the basic perspicuity—or clarity—of Scripture, we also have taken to heart Paul's admonition to Timothy: "Do your best to present yourself to God as one approved, a worker who has no need to be ashamed, rightly handling the word of truth" (2 Tim. 2:15). Therefore, understanding what the Bible says, and what it means, takes *work*.

But a lifetime spent in the halls of academia is not necessary for a better understanding of God's Word (though it can certainly help). Any Christian can learn to understand and apply Scripture in a way that is both intellectually and spiritually healthy. While many good books have been written about hermeneutics, this short appendix will give you some basic tools to get started—enriching and sharpening your understanding of the Bible's prophecies.

Context

There are several principles of interpretation to keep in mind when looking at Scripture. The first and key principle of hermeneutics is that "context is king." When reading a verse or passage, we need to look at how it fits into its context: "the parts of a written or spoken statement that precede or follow a specific **word** or passage, usually **influencing its** meaning or effect: *You have misinterpreted my remark because you took it out of context.*"[2]

To avoid misinterpreting a Scripture, we need to look at its context in several dimensions:

- the immediate context (the paragraph or section in which a verse or passage appears)
- the larger context (the chapter)
- the Bible book
- the Bible as a whole

Understanding where the verse or passage fits in these various dimensions of context helps us interpret it better. We ought always to read the Word with the context in mind. Failure to do so can lead to ungrounded or even fanciful interpretations.

Other Principles

Beyond context, the biblical interpreter must keep in mind other basic principles, best covered in other volumes.[3] These include understanding human language, setting, word study, thought structure, figurative language, parables, poetry, the unity of Scripture, the coherence of truth, how to handle apparent discrepancies, the intended audience, and the intended response. It sounds like a lot to learn, but isn't rightly handling the word of truth worth it?

Essential Tools

You'll need a few essentials: a good study Bible (I recommend the majestic *ESV Study Bible*, also available online), a basic commentary, a Bible dictionary, a good volume of systematic theology, a theological dictionary, a Bible atlas, and a concordance, for starters. Some of my favorites are in the notes.

BibleGateway.com, hosted by Zondervan, provides a great way to look up verses and passages in almost any English translation. The Biblios Online Parallel Bible (http://bible.cc/) allows you to look up individual verses in multiple translations, and it includes insights from classic commentaries (often quoted in this book).

Here are a few more resources to help you get started on this challenging, but ultimately satisfying, hermeneutical journey:

- Gleason Archer, *A Survey of Old Testament Introduction* (Chicago: Moody, 2007). Who wrote what, when, why, and to whom—Part 1.
- Gleason Archer, *New Encyclopedia of Bible Difficulties* (Grand Rapids: Zondervan, 2001). Got a troubling question about the Bible? Chances are you'll find the answer here.
- G. K. Beale and D. A. Carson, eds., *Commentary on the New Testament Use of the Old Testament* (Downers Grove, IL: InterVarsity, 2007). Densely written, but it will show you how New Testament authors interpreted the Old as pointing to Christ.
- Gordon D. Fee and Douglas Stuart, *How to Read the Bible for All Its Worth* (Grand Rapids: Zondervan, 2009). A standard, readable, and proven work.
- Donald Guthrie (no relation), *New Testament Introduction*, rev. ed. (Downers Grove, IL: InterVarsity, 1990). Who wrote what, when, why, and to whom—Part 2.
- Robertson McQuilkin, *Understanding and Applying the Bible: An Introduction to Hermeneutics*, rev. ed. (Chicago: Moody, 2009). The volume that got me going on a solid hermeneutical path.
- Leland Ryken, *Understanding English Bible Translation: The Case for an Essentially Literal Approach* (Wheaton: Crossway, 2009). As opposed to translations that are more of a paraphrase.
- R. C. Sproul, *Knowing Scripture*, rev. ed. (Downers Grove, IL: InterVarsity Press, 2009). One of my favorite writers and preachers offers solid hermeneutical help.

Appendix 2

Different Approaches to Interpreting Prophecy

I followed some basic hermeneutical principles when handling the prophecies in this volume. I outline them here, followed by a brief examination of the major schools of Bible prophecy interpretation.

1. *Unless the evidence clearly says otherwise, assume that a prophecy had some meaning to the people who originally heard or read it.* The Bible is not a codebook of mysterious utterances, such as the *Prophecies of Nostradamus*. A Bible prophecy usually was not unintelligible to the people in the original audience.

2. *A prophecy, all things being equal, speaks both to the time it is written and to the future.* A prophecy, while speaking about future events, is meant to change the lives of its hearers *today*—a key assumption of this book. As Robertson McQuilkin has said, "The chief purpose is to affect the conduct of those who hear the prophecy. Another purpose is only met only when the prophecy is fulfilled. That purpose is to build faith, to establish confidence in the God who miraculously foretold events."[1]

3. *Bible prophecies are sometimes, but not always, best understood in hindsight.* The prophecy, "Out of Egypt I called my son," for example, initially referred to the nation of Israel but was later fulfilled in Jesus Christ (see chapter 37, "Called Out of Egypt"). Few people looking at this Old Testament statement at the time it was made could have imagined it also spoke of the coming Messiah.

4. *Generally prophecies are meant to be understood, not concealed.*[2] The Book of Revelation, for example, while difficult to understand for many twenty-first-century readers, employs a literary genre that

was well-known to first-century readers—apocalyptic literature.[3] As the angel told John (and us), "Do not seal up the words of the prophecy of this book, for the time is near" (Rev. 22:10).

5. *We are in a better position to understand prophetic fulfillment than many of the prophets, whose view of the future was partial.* God's revelation in Scripture is progressive and unfolding. Not everyone knew everything all at once. As Jesus told his listeners (and us), "For truly, I say to you, many prophets and righteous people longed to see what you see, and did not see it, and to hear what you hear, and did not hear it" (Matt. 13:17).

The Main Schools of Bible Prophecy

In this book I have tried to come at the prophecies fresh, without preconceived notions. I wanted to let them speak to me as if I were in the original audience. I have tried not to fit them into any particular prophetic cubbyhole. The reader will be the best judge as to whether I have succeeded.

Nevertheless we need to approach the prophecies with our eyes open. Generally an interpreter will see them through some sort of theological system. This is not wrong; we just need to be aware of his or her particular approach to eschatology (the study of last things) and see how it accords with Scripture and sound hermeneutics.

Theologian Millard Erickson says we should ask a series of questions of any system (and, I would add, of this book) that purports to interpret the prophecies:[4]

1. Does it view eschatology as describing the future or the current day?
   a. The futuristic view says most of the prophecies are about the future.
   b. The preterist view says most of the prophecies dealt with events in the lifetime of the writer.
   c. The historical view says that while the prophecies were in the future for the prophet, they are fulfilled in the history of the church.
   d. The symbolic or idealist view says that prophecies refer to timeless truths, not to historical events.

2. Is the view of earth's future mainly optimistic or pessimistic?
3. Is God the primary mover of events in the last days, or are human beings?
4. Does it see God's promises as being fulfilled primarily here on the earth or in heaven?
5. Are the promises mostly for the church or also for the world?
6. Do the benefits of the new age come to us as individuals or as a group?
7. Does it reserve a special place for the Jewish people?

Erickson takes special note of the eschatology of dispensationalism.[5] He describes several features of this approach:

- A unified interpretative system made popular by the Scofield Reference Bible (and later writers, such as Hal Lindsey)
- Literal interpretation of Scripture
- "Israel" in prophecy always means national or ethnic Israel, not the church
- Belief that God has managed the world and salvation history through a series of "dispensations," or stages of God's revelation and working (for example, dispensations of innocence, of conscience, of human government, of promise, of law, and of grace, with the final dispensation yet to come)
- An emphasis on and a particular way of interpreting purported future events and figures, such as the rapture, the Antichrist, the great tribulation, and the millennium

Different systems have particular strengths and weaknesses. As you work through the prophecies for yourself, it is good to keep these approaches in mind and test them according to sound hermeneutics and the leading of the Holy Spirit.

While Christians will disagree about which of these approaches (or some combination thereof) represents the best way to interpret the Bible's prophecies, in the end we will agree with scholars F. F. Bruce and J. J. Scott Jr.: "The eschatological outlook of the [New Testament] is well summed up in the words: 'Christ Jesus our hope' (1 Tim. 1:1)."[6]

Notes

Introduction

1. Hugh Ross, "Fulfilled Prophecy: Evidence for the Reliability of the Bible," Reasons to Believe, http://www.reasons. org/fulfilled-prophecy-evidence-reliability-bible.

2. For more on the accuracy and trustworthiness of the Bible, see Josh McDowell, *The New Evidence That Demands a Verdict* (Nashville: Thomas Nelson, 1999).

Chapter 4 Blessings and Curses

1. Rob Zaretsky, "No. 1964: Lisbon Earthquake," *Engines of Our Ingenuity*, University of Houston, November 1964, http://www.uh.edu/engines/epi1964.htm.

Chapter 5 Elijah's Drought

1. Justin Taylor, ed., *ESV Study Bible*, note on 1 Kings 17:1 (Wheaton: Crossway, 2008), 632.

Chapter 6 Judgment against Israel

1. John D. Currid and David P. Barrett, *ESV Bible Atlas* (Wheaton: Crossway, 2010), 158–59.

Chapter 7 Judgment against Jerusalem and the Babylonian Captivity

1. Walter A. Elwell, ed., *Baker Encyclopedia of the Bible* (Grand Rapids: Baker, 1988), 1:1061.

Chapter 8 The Seventy Weeks

1. Taylor, *ESV Study Bible*, note on Matthew 24:15, 1873.

Chapter 9 Return via Cyrus

1. Jack Finegan, *Light from the Ancient Past: The Archaeological Background of the Hebrew-Christian Religion* (Princeton University Press, 1946), 191.

2. Currid and Barrett, *ESV Bible Atlas*, 179.

3. See Jeremiah 25:12.

Chapter 10 The New Covenant

1. Mendy Hecht, "The 613 Commandments," Jewish Beliefs, Chabad.org, http://www.chabad.org/library/article_cdo/aid/756399/jewish/The-613–Commandments.htm.

Chapter 13 Nineveh

1. Finegan, *Light from the Ancient Past*, 172.

2. Ibid., 172–73.

Chapter 14 Syria

1. *Syria* as used in this book is not the same as the modern nation-state of the same name, although there is some overlap of territory.

2. Elwell, *Baker Encyclopedia of the Bible*, 2:2010.

3. Ibid., 2:2010–11.

4. Taylor, *ESV Study Bible*, note on Amos 1:3, 1659.

5. Ibid.

6. Finegan, *Light from the Ancient Past*, 174.

Chapter 15 Tyre's Watery Doom

1. Much of the following description of the Phoenicians and Tyre relies on R. A. Guisepi, ed., "The Phoenicians," History World International, http://history-world. org/phoenicians.htm; and also Taylor, *ESV Study Bible*, notes on Ezekiel 26 (various), 1537–38.

Chapter 16 Nineveh's Judgment

1. Much of the following description of Assyrian military might relies on Ernest Volkman, *Science Goes to War: The Search for the Ultimate Weapon, from Greek Fire to Star Wars* (New York: John Wiley: 2002), 20–23.

2. Much of the following description of Nineveh relies on Currid and Barrett, *ESV Bible Atlas*, 156.

3. Taylor, *ESV Study Bible*, "Introduction to Nahum: Date," 1709.

4. Currid and Barrett, *ESV Bible Atlas*, 156, 170.

Chaper 17 Edom Brought Low

1. See Genesis 25–36 for the story of Jacob and Esau, and also chapter 2 in this book, "Jacob Returns."

2. Elwell, *Baker Encyclopedia of the Bible*, 1:656.

3. Josh McDowell, *Evidence That Demands a Verdict* (San Bernardino: Here's Life, 1979), 290.

4. John H. Walton, *The Minor Prophets, Job, Psalms, Proverbs, Ecclesiastes, Song of Songs*, vol. 5 of *Zondervan Illustrated Bible Backgrounds Commentary* (Grand Rapids: Zondervan, 2009), 92.

Chapter 18 Philistia

1. For much of this chapter's description of the Philistines, see Elwell, *Baker*

Encyclopedia of the Bible, 2:1681–1682. See also http://en.wikipedia.org/wiki/Ramesses _III. The modern-day Palestinians, who are largely Muslims or Christians, bear no relation to the ancient, pagan Philistines.

2. "Caphtor," Jewish Virtual Library, http://www.jewishvirtuallibrary.org/jsource /judaica/ejud_0002_0004_0_03927.html.

3. Taylor, *ESV Study Bible*, notes on Jer. 47:1 and 47:1–7, 1454–55.

4. Elwell, *Baker Encyclopedia of the Bible*, 2:1684.

Chapter 19 Ammon

1. For much of this description of the Ammonites see Elwell, *Baker Encyclopedia of the Bible*, 1:71–74; see also Paul Lawrence, *The IVP Atlas of Bible History* (Downers Grove, IL: InterVarsity, 2006), 80.

2. Taylor, *ESV Study Bible*, note on Ezek. 25:4, 1536.

Chapter 20 Moab

1. See chapter 19, "Ammon: Actions and Attitudes."

2. Taylor, *ESV Study Bible*, "Jeremiah Prophesies against Moab," 1455.

3. Ibid., note on Amos 2:1–3, 1661.

Chapter 21 Egypt

1. Finegan, *Light from the Ancient Past*, 87.

2. Currid and Barrett, *ESV Bible Atlas*, 167, 170.

3. Finegan, *Light from the Ancient Past*, 115.

Chapter 22 Nebuchadnezzar's Dream of Earthly Empires

1. William Shakespeare, *Henry the Fourth*, part 2, act 3, scene 1.

2. Walter A. Elwell, *Evangelical Commentary on the Bible* (Grand Rapids: Baker, 1989), 593.

Chapter 23 Nebuchadnezzar

1. See chapter 22, "Nebuchadnezzar's Dream of Earthly Empires."

2. Elwell, *Evangelical Commentary on the Bible*, 594.

3. Ibid., 595.

Chapter 24 Babylon

1. See chapter 23, "Nebuchadnezzar: A Beastly Judgment."

2. Finegan, *Light from the Ancient Past*, 186.

3. Ibid.

4. Ibid, 189–90.

5. In 1983, Saddam Hussein began to rebuild Babylon on top of its ancient ruins. Imitating Nebuchadnezzar, Saddam had his name inscribed on many of the bricks. In 2003 he was preparing to have a cable car built over the site when the U.S. invasion began. After he was overthrown, the work stopped. Authorities, however, have reopened the site to tourists. See "Babylon, Reconstruction" at http://en.wikipedia.org/wiki/Babylon#Archaeology.

Chapter 25 The Nations to Be Blessed

1. See Q.1 at http://www.reformed.org/documents/WSC.html.

2. For God's prophecy of judgment on the antediluvian world, see Genesis 6:7.

3. Jason Mandryk, *Operation World: The Definitive Prayer Guide to Every Nation*, 7th ed. (Colorado Springs: Biblica, 2010), 5.

Chapter 26 A Great King

1. In Acts 4:25–26, for example, they applied Psalm 2 to Jesus.

Chapter 27 An Unending Royal Line

1. John H. Walton, *Chronological and Background Charts of the Old Testament* (Grand Rapids: Zondervan, 1978), 59.

2. "The Kings of Judah," *Jewish Virtual Library*, http://www.jewishvirtual-library.org/jsource/History/Judah.html.

3. Mark Driscoll and Gerry Breshears, *Doctrine: What Christians Should Believe* (Wheaton: Crossway, 2010), 176–77.

Chapter 29 A Future David

1. "Isaiah 4:2," *Barnes' Notes on the Bible*, http://bible.cc/isaiah/4–2.htm.

Chapter 30 The Son of Man Given Dominion

1. Elwell, *Baker Encyclopedia of the Bible*, 2:1983.

2. Seen by many as an explication of Daniel's earlier prophecy concerning Nebuchadnezzar's dream of earthly empires (see chapter 22); see also Taylor, *ESV Study Bible*, note on Dan. 7:3, 1599.

Chapter 31 The Virgin Birth of God

1. One spurious (and longstanding) charge was that Mary became pregnant by a Roman soldier named Panthera. See, for example, Peter Schafer, *Jesus in the Talmud* (Princeton: Princeton University Press, 2007), 19–20.

2. G. K. Beale and D. A. Carson, eds., *Commentary on the New Testament Use of the Old Testament* (Grand Rapids: Baker, 2007), 4; see also Isa. 8:3.

Chapter 32 The Star

1. Elwell, *Baker Encyclopedia of the Bible*, 2:1999.

2. Ibid.

3. Beale and Carson, eds., *Commentary on the New Testament Use of the Old Testament*, 8.

4. "Setting the Stage," *The Star of Bethlehem*, http://www.bethlehemstar.net/stage/stage.htm.

5. Ibid.

6. Elwell, *Baker Encyclopedia of the Bible*, 2:1999–2000.

Chapter 33 Born in Bethlehem

1. Taylor, *ESV Study Bible*, note on Luke 2:3–4, 1947.

2. Elwell, *Baker Encyclopedia of the Bible*, 1:289–90.

3. "Organization of the Twelve Tribes of Israel," http://www.israel-a-history-of.com/twelve-tribes-of-israel.html#%3Cb%3EThe%20Clan%3C/b%3E.

Chapter 34 Simeon and Anna

1. Most scholars believe the Magi came later, when Jesus was living in a house (Matt. 2:11). Supporting this view is the fact that when Herod slaughtered the male children in Bethlehem in an effort to murder the king of the Jews, he ordered the deaths of boys "who were two years old or under" (Matt. 2:16–18).

Chapter 35 Kings Will Bring Him Gifts

1. "Everybody's Favorites: Hymns That Last," *Christianity Today*, March 2011, 31, http://www.christianitytoday.com/ct/special/pdf/110307-hymnsthatlast.pdf.

2. Isaac Watts, "Jesus Shall Reign," selected verses quoted in *The Cyber Hymnal*, http://www.cyberhymnal.org/htm/j/s/jsreign.htm.

3. Quoted in *The Cyber Hymnal*, http://www.cyberhymnal.org/htm/j/s/jsreign.htm.

Chapter 36 Slaughter of the Innocents

1. Beale and Carson, eds., *Commentary on the New Testament Use of the Old Testament*, 3–11.

2. Ibid., 8–9; see chapter 10, "The New Covenant," for a discussion of Jeremiah's prophecy of the new covenant.

3. See chapter 52, "The Seed versus the Serpent," for a discussion of the enmity between the serpent and the Son of Eve.

Chapter 37 Called Out of Egypt

1. See previous two chapters.

2. See, for example, chapter 6, "Judgment against Israel."

3. R. T. France, *The Gospel according to Matthew*, Tyndale New Testament Commentary (Grand Rapids: Eerdmans, 1985), 40, quoted in Beale and Carson, eds., *Commentary on the New Testament Use of the Old Testament*, 8.

4. Beale and Carson, eds., *Commentary on the New Testament Use of the Old Testament*, 8.

Chapter 38 Elijah's Return

1. See chapter 5, "Elijah's Drought."

Chapter 39 "The Spirit of the Lord Is upon Me"

1. Adrian Curtis, *Oxford Bible Atlas*, 4th ed. (Oxford: Oxford University Press, 2007), 149.

2. For example, Beale and Carson, eds., *Commentary on the New Testament Use of the Old Testament*, 288.

3. *Gill's Exposition of the Entire Bible*, quoted at http://bible.cc/luke/4–18.htm.

4. See chapter 38, "Elijah's Return."

Chapter 40 "Zeal for Your House Will Consume Me"

1. "Zeal," *Merriam-Webster Dictionary*, http://www.merriam-webster.com/dictionary/zeal.

2. Scholars, however, are divided over whether the scene at the temple in John 2 is the same as Jesus's cleansing of the temple in Matthew 21, Mark 11, and Luke 19, or instead is an earlier event in his ministry.

3. Quoted in Stan Guthrie, "The Controversial Tim Tebow," Crosswalk.com, Nov. 30, 2011, http://www.crosswalk.com/news/the-controversial-tim-tebow.html.

4. See also Matt. 26:61 for a garbling of this prophecy by his opponents. Also see the section "Jesus—Death and Resurrection" later in this book.

Chapter 41 Miracle Worker

1. Quotes in this section about the blind man are taken from John 9.

Chapter 42 "God Will Raise Up a Prophet Like Me from among Your Brothers"

1. Joseph Telushkin, *Jewish Literacy* (New York: William Morrow, 1991), quoted in "Moses," *Jewish Virtual Library*, http://www.jewishvirtuallibrary.org/jsource/biography/moses.html.

2. See Taylor, *ESV Study Bible*, "Introduction to the Prophetic Books," 1229–32.

Chapter 43 The Cornerstone

1. Quoted at http://bible.cc/psalms /118–22.htm.

2. Taylor, *ESV Study Bible*, note on Psalm 118:22–23, 1092.

3. See *Gill's Exposition of the Entire Bible*, quoted at http://bible.cc/psalms/118–22 .htm.

4. See chapter 1, "Blessed to Be a Blessing."

Chapter 44 Riding a Donkey

1. Flavius Josephus, *The Wars of the Jews*, book VII, chap. V, par. 4, quoted from http://unix.luc.edu/~avande1/jeru-salem/sources/titus-triumphal-procession. htm.

2. Elwell, *Baker Encyclopedia of the Bible*, 1:93.

Chapter 46 The Sign of Jonah

1. See chapter 13, "Nineveh: Threat-ened and Spared."

Chapter 48 "Strike the Shepherd and the Sheep Will Be Scattered"

1. Winston Churchill, quoted in *The History Place*, Great Speeches Collection, http://www.historyplace.com/speeches/ churchill.htm.

2. See chapter 44, "Riding a Donkey."

Chapter 49 "You Will Deny Me Three Times"

1. Elwell, *Baker Encyclopedia of the Bible*, 2:1661.

Chapter 50 "You Will Not Abandon My Soul to the Grave"

1. N. T. Wright, "Jesus' Resurrection and Christian Origins," http://www.ntwright page.com/Wright_Jesus_Resurrection.htm.

2. Ibid.

3. References suggested by N. T. Wright.

4. See chapter 49, "You Will Deny Me Three Times."

Chapter 51 Isaiah's Vision

1. Wright, "Jesus' Resurrection and Christian Origins," emphasis in original.

Chapter 53 "Proclaimed throughout the Whole World"

1. See chapter 1, "Blessed to Be a Blessing."

2. Mandryk, *Operation World, 5*.

Chapter 54 The Outpouring of the Spirit

1. Keil and Delitzsch, *Biblical Commentary on the Old Testament*, quoted at http://bible.cc/deuteronomy/6–4.htm.

Chapter 55 "I Will Build My Church"

1. See chapter 30, "The Son of Man Given Dominion."

2. See chapter 49, "You Will Deny Me Three Times."

3. The Greek word translated as "church" is *ekklesia*, meaning God's called out community of followers.

4. Robert H. Brom, "The Great Heresies," *Catholic Answers*, http://www.catholic .com/tracts/the-great-heresies. Unfortu-nately, this otherwise helpful and informa-tive Catholic resource lists Protestantism as a heresy.

Chapter 56 The Destruction of the Temple

1. Taylor, *ESV Study Bible*, "Herod's Temple in the Time of Jesus," 1943.

2. Flavius Josephus, *The Wars of the Jews*, book XV, chap. XI, par. 1, quoted from http://www.ccel.org/j/josephus/works /ant-15.htm.

3. See chapter 44, "Riding a Donkey."

4. Tacitus, *Histories*, "Fragments," no. 2, quoted at http://penelope.uchicago.edu/ Thayer/E/Roman/Texts/Tacitus/Histories/ Fragments*.html#2.

5. But see chapter 11, "All Israel Will Be Saved," which describes Israel's future.

6. "The Temple of Herod," *International Standard Bible Encyclopedia*, at http://www.bible-history.com/jewish temple/JEWISH_TEMPLEInternational _Standard_Bible_Enc.htm.

7. "Western Wall," http://www.bible places.com/westernwall.htm.

Chapter 57 The Second Coming

1. C. S. Lewis, *The Last Battle* (New York: HarperCollins, 2000), 173.

2. See chapter 56, "The Destruction of the Temple."

3. See for example, chapter 37, "Called Out of Egypt," and 42, "God Will Raise Up a Prophet Like Me from among Your Brothers."

4. Flavius Josephus, quoted at "The Romans Destroy the Temple at Jerusalem, 70 AD," http://www.eyewitnesstohistory.com/ jewishtemple.htm.

Chapter 58 No One Knows the Day or the Hour

1. Some students of Bible prophecy say that God will suddenly "rapture" his people from the earth prior to the Great Tribulation, a time of unprecedented suffering before Christ returns to set up his kingdom.

2. David Morgan, "Rapture Predictor Harold Camping Suffers Stroke," http:// www.cbsnews.com/stories/2011/06/13/ national/main20070762.shtml.

3. Anonymous, "Harold Camping Apologizes for Faulty Rapture Predictions and Retires, Report States," http://www. huffingtonpost.com/2011/11/01/harold -camping-apologizes-rapture-predictions _n_1069520.html.

Chapter 59 The Last Judgment

1. To see it online, go to Art and the Bible, http://www.artbible.info/art/large/54. html.

2. "Existence of the General Judgment," *Catholic Encyclopedia*," quoted at http:// www.newadvent.org/cathen/08552a.htm.

3. But see Matthew 12:37, which says we will also be judged based on our *words*.

4. See chapter 51, "Isaiah's Vision," and 52, "The Seed versus the Serpent."

5. Dietrich Bonhoeffer, *The Cost of Discipleship*, 2nd ed. (New York: Macmillan, 1959), 69, emphasis in original.

6. See Revelation 20:11–15.

Appendix 1

1. "Hermeneutics," *Catholic Encyclopedia*, http://www.newadvent.org/ cathen/07271a.htm.

2. "Context," first definition, *Dictionary.com*, http://dictionary.reference.com/ browse/context.

3. For the brief listing that follows, I am indebted to Robertson McQuilkin, *Understanding and Applying the Bible: An Introduction to Hermeneutics* (Chicago: Moody, 1983). A revised and expanded 2009 edition is now available.

Appendix 2

1. McQuilkin, *Understanding and Applying the Bible*, 215.

2. The prophecy in Daniel 12 was meant to be concealed, however. See verse 4.

3. For a good description of apocalyptic literature, see John W. Carter, "An Introduction to the Interpretation of Apocalyptic Literature," *The American Journal of Biblical Theology*, http://www.biblicaltheology.com/Research/CarterJ08.pdf.

4. Adapted from Millard J. Erickson, *Christian Theology* (Grand Rapids: Baker, 1985), 1154–55.

5. Adapted from ibid., 1162–64.

6. Walter A. Elwell, ed., *Evangelical Dictionary of Theology*, 2nd ed. (Grand Rapids: Baker, 2001), 389.

Stan Guthrie (BS, Journalism, University of Florida; Certificate in Biblical Studies, and MA, Intercultural Studies, Columbia International University) came to Christ in high school after reading about fulfilled prophecy. He is the author of *All That Jesus Asks: How His Questions Can Teach and Transform Us* and *Missions in the Third Millennium: 21 Key Trends in the 21st Century.* He is also coauthor (with Jerry Root) of *The Sacrament of Evangelism.* Stan, a book editor and literary agent, hosts the *Books & Culture* podcasts and writes opinion pieces for Break Point.org and Crosswalk.com. A *Christianity Today* editor at large, he blogs at *StanGuthrie.com.*

Stan is married to Christine, and they have three children.

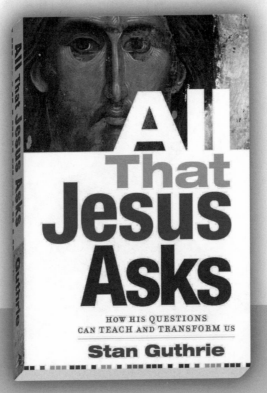